BRISTOL

THE PHOTOGRAPHIC COLLECTION

Ships' masts, warehouses and ancient churches – the centre of Bristol with the tower of St Stephen's
church an enduring landmark in an ever changing city; here the church is seen in May 1858, prior to
restoration in 1860–61. The stone warehouses on Broad Quay were occupied by Dunlop, Mackie & Co.,
wine, spirit and porter merchants until about 1880. (J.W.G. Gutch)

BRISTOL

THE PHOTOGRAPHIC COLLECTION

DAVID J. EVELEIGH

SUTTON PUBLISHING

This edition first published in 2003 by
Sutton Publishing Limited · Phoenix Mill
Thrupp · Stroud · Gloucestershire · GL5 2BU

Bristol 1850–1919 was first published in 1996 by Sutton Publishing Limited
Bristol 1920–1969 was first published in 1998 by Sutton Publishing Limited

British Library Cataloguing in Publication Data
A catalogue record for this book is available from the British Library.

ISBN 0 7509 3353 4

Typeset in 10/12 Perpetua.
Typesetting and origination by
Sutton Publishing Limited.
Printed and bound in Great Britain by
J.H. Haynes & Co. Ltd, Sparkford.

CONTENTS

Part One – Bristol 1850–1919

Part Two – 1920–1969

Part One
Bristol 1850–1919

INTRODUCTION

In 1908 the *Western Daily Press* ran a series of articles in the company's *Evening News* charting the progress made in the city since the 1850s. The following year the articles appeared as a single volume entitled *Bristol As It Was – And As It Is* and it was clear to its author, George Frederick Stone, that the progress achieved in that fifty-year span was unprecedented and quite unlike the slow, organic development that had previously characterised the city. Bristol had, in short, experienced a comprehensive and dramatic transformation: the making of the modern city.

The photographs featured here coincide with this crucial phase in the creation of modern Bristol from the 1850s to the time of the First World War. In 1850 Bristol preserved the appearance of a late Georgian city with abundant remains from earlier phases in its history. Fragments of the city walls and castle survived as reminders of the city's medieval origins along with the towers of the old parish churches which rose above narrow streets of picturesque, gabled houses of the seventeenth century. The port and city were inextricably mixed: ships' masts were to be seen amongst the city streets – a sight that never failed to impress visitors – and much of the city's commercial life depended on coastal and overseas trade. The Bristol of 1850 was also dirty, insanitary and desperately short of clean drinking water. In 1845 sanitary inspectors had found in Bristol some of the worst living conditions in England and the third highest death rate.

In the decades that followed, the Victorians were to transform the physical environment of the city. The churches, mostly, survived – they were, of course, an essential part of the Victorian city – but much else was swept away with little sentiment and scant regard for conservation in a process of modernisation which established much of Bristol's present-day appearance and character. Narrow city thoroughfares were widened and timber-framed houses replaced with new factories, offices and shops. Fortunately, some old buildings lost as early as the 1850s, such as the Fourteen Stars Tavern, Counterslip, were recorded by camera before demolition. Streets were cleaned, sewers laid and lighting improved, first with gas and then electricity. An efficient urban transport system was established, local newspapers proliferated for an increasingly literate population and telephones made their debut – in 1879. In addition, a wide range of public services and amenities was introduced: from schools and hospitals to libraries, public baths and parks.

None of this, of course, was unique to Bristol: cities and towns throughout Britain were undergoing a similar process of modernisation. In Bristol, as elsewhere, it was a process often muddled and fumbling, achieved through an uneasy alliance of private enterprise and municipal intervention. Bristol was notable in that several major utilities, such as the supply of gas, water and the tramways, were in the hands of commercial concerns; nevertheless, this period marks the growing role of civic administration in determining the affairs of the city. From 1848 the docks were placed under municipal control and the generation of electricity (apart from the tramway's supply) was in the hands of the City Corporation. From the 1850s new committees charged with responsibility for public health and sanitation, education, cemeteries, open spaces and so forth were created, sometimes taking over functions previously vested in the old parish authorities, or often managing new areas – such as library provision – the result of national legislation.

Civic administration was thus extended citywide as the city itself rapidly widened its boundaries. Mid-nineteenth century maps show that the city's layout still related closely to the medieval plan. But after 1850, like other Victorian cities, Bristol rapidly expanded, aided by trains and trams, engulfing nearby farms and neighbouring villages. The suburbs were differentiated socially: the industrial areas of housing built to the east and south of the city acquired a very different character to the fashionable suburbs of Clifton, Cotham and Redland in the west and north. The expansion was accompanied by boundary changes in 1894, 1897 and 1904, adding more than 12,000 acres to its municipal area whilst the population grew by 222,000. These figures hide the experiences of thousands of individual Bristolians who lived through and contributed to this period of change, and whilst the part played by leading citizens – Sir George White, Joseph Storrs Fry and others – is well documented their achievements can overshadow the lives of many ordinary citizens.

This book, however, draws attention to some lesser-known Bristolians: James Cox, for example, blinded in a foundry explosion and as a result convinced of his duty to preach the word of God; William Bailey, a haulier from St Philip's Marsh who played his small part in distributing the remains of the city's horse population – once they had been boiled, ground and crushed – as manure and glue; a social contrast is provided by Dorothy and Frances Brewer, daughters of an accountant in the affluent suburb of Cotham, seen with their toy horse and dolls in about 1910. The prim figure on the left of the 1890s photograph in Blue Maids Orphanage on page 115 is almost certainly Isolene Lee, the matron of the orphanage, and the woman with her is probably the schoolmistress, Ann Miller.

The survival of old photographs is largely a matter of chance and to some extent the availability of surviving photographs has determined the shape of this book. Some of the views are published here for the first time, but in order to achieve a balanced representation it has proved impossible to exclude some well-known views. Where the name of the photographer is known this is added at the end of the caption in brackets, and each picture is placed in the context of the main theme of this book – the making of the modern city of Bristol.

THE INNER CITY

The idea of an inner city was a consequence of nineteenth-century urban expansion. As Bristol acquired new suburbs, each with its own identity and character, the old city came to be known as the 'central district' or the 'ancient city'. The city had originated in Saxon times around a bridge over the Avon; the Saxon name was 'Brigstow' – the place of a bridge. The medieval city had developed between the Avon and Frome: a huddle of narrow streets in a cluster of parishes, some tiny, like All Saints', and each marked by a church tower creating one of the distinctive architectural features of the inner city.

The medieval town centred on the intersection of four main streets: the High Street and Broad Street, Corn Street and Wine Street. A High Cross stood at this junction until removed in 1733, although by the nineteenth century it no longer served as the centre. Indeed, it is a peculiarity of Bristol that it does not have a single, undisputed central focus. The new Victorian towns and cities of the midlands and north were designed around a physical centre, usually a square dominated by a town hall which clearly marked the town or city centre and asserted the supremacy of civic authority. Bristol's Council House – until the completion of the present building on College Green – was tucked away in Corn Street close to other prominent commercial buildings such as the Corn Exchange. Rather, Bristol had several focal points: Corn Street as the chief commercial street was one, the quayside in St Augustine's Reach another and in the late 1890s, when part of this was covered over, Bristol acquired the Tramway Centre: a raised triangle of pavement where the trams stopped. For a few decades this was Bristol's centre; but it was not a monument to civic authority – rather the centre of operations for the independently owned tramway company run by Sir George White – a frequent protagonist of the City Corporation!

Nevertheless, it was not privately run trams but the publicly owned City Dock that gave the centre its atmosphere and character. The non-tidal Floating Harbour – 83 acres in extent – which enabled ships to float at all times, rather than sink in the mud at low tide, had been completed by the independent dock company in 1809. Unfortunately, high port dues were charged to recoup the investment, making this one of the most expensive ports in the country. As ship owners turned to other ports with more competitive dues, public agitation found a powerful voice in the Free Port Association which, in 1848, succeeded in transferring the operation of the port to the Bristol Corporation. Immediately, the city introduced more moderate dues but the port continued to decline owing to the introduction of ever larger iron ships which could neither navigate the tortuous course of the Avon nor enter the Floating Harbour. In 1873 the entrance locks at the Cumberland Basin were enlarged but it was clear that, if Bristol was to continue to function as a major port, new deep water docks were essential. 'Dockisation' of the entire length of the Avon down river from Bristol was seriously contemplated but the ultimate solution was the creation of new docks initially run by private companies at the mouth of the Avon. In 1877 new deep water docks were opened at Avonmouth, followed two years later by a dock at Portishead.

In 1884 control of the new docks at the mouth of the Avon passed to the Docks Committee. It was here that the bulk of Bristol's ocean-going trade came to be concentrated. The decline of the City Docks, however, was a gradual process and throughout the rest of the nineteenth century tall-masted sailing ships could be found berthed in the heart of the city. To the usual scenes of street life could be added the fascinating spectacle of the forest of ships' masts, rigging and all the paraphernalia – warehouses, cranes and cargoes – of docking, rubbing shoulders with fashionable shops and ancient churches. The course of the Frome, realigned in the thirteenth century to provide improved berthing, brought ships as far as Stone Bridge, near St Mary-on-the-Quay. Here, in St Augustine's Reach, ships trading with Africa, the West Indies and America were crowded, unloading cargoes of raw materials: corn, tobacco, sugar cane and luxury goods such as tea and coffee which supplied the city's trades and industries. A few streets away, along the old course of the Avon as far as Bristol Bridge, tall-masted vessels could be found berthed at Welsh Back and Redcliffe Back, two old-established quays traditionally associated with the coastal trade of the Bristol Channel and South Wales. The names 'Welsh Back' and the 'Llandoger Trow' are reminders of this once important trade; the term 'Back' is believed to refer to the backs of merchants' houses which formerly lined the quayside. By the mid-nineteenth century the merchants had long since departed for more salubrious surroundings and the backs were chiefly lined with granaries, flour mills and other industrial premises.

Although the City Docks were in decline, developments still took place in the second half of the nineteenth century. A new corporation granary was built by the Docks Committee in 1887 overlooking St Augustine's Reach. New deep water berths were constructed at Princes Wharf and Whapping Wharf and given railway connections; further new stone quays were constructed at Dean's Marsh and around to Canon's Marsh. Smaller steamships also became a regular feature of the City Docks after 1850, and operating fast, regular schedules around the British Isles created a need for transit sheds where cargoes could be swiftly prepared and dispatched. Dublin Shed was built on Narrow Quay and 'E' Shed, designed by Edward Gabriel in 1894, was given an ornate elevation and iron gates facing St Augustine's Parade.

Whilst the docks contributed to the changing face of the inner city during the late nineteenth century, there were other more decisive factors at work. Foremost was the increasing volume of road traffic. Victorian and Edwardian photographs of Bristol show streets filled with a chaotic variety of traffic: hand carts, barrows and small horse-drawn delivery vans; then the larger horse-drawn carts, wagons and drays, and passenger vehicles including private carriages and vehicles for hire – two-wheeled hansom cabs and the more sedate four-wheeled growlers. As the city's population grew, traffic across the central area increased: from the 1870s tramlines added to the congestion along some routes and by the end of the century there were also hundreds of 'safety' bicycles on the roads. The old city streets, in many instances, were simply not wide enough to accommodate the extra traffic and their layout did not reflect the predominant flow. Nowhere was this more apparent than along the route from Clifton to the railway terminus at Temple Meads. The railway station opened in 1840 – rather out on a limb – east of the centre, and created extra traffic which was hampered by several restrictions. Attempts to improve the route to Temple Meads began soon after the station opened. As early as 1845 the Corporation proposed to construct a new thoroughfare to be called Victoria Street and to widen Bristol Bridge. Municipal resolve faltered at the cost and it was not until 1859 that work began on widening the east side of Bristol Bridge; Victoria Street followed in 1871, cutting through old property in Temple and Redcliffe; and then in 1873–4 the western side of the bridge was widened. The following year the Corporation decided to extend Baldwin Street, creating a straighter route between the Drawbridge and Bristol Bridge and alleviating pressure on Corn Street and Clare Street. The scheme went ahead in spite of opposition from 'influential citizens', who owned property in the way of the new road, and was opened with full civic pomp and ceremony on 1 March 1881. 'There are few Bristol thoroughfares', wrote Stone in 1909, 'on which fifty years have produced greater changes than Baldwin Street – practically the whole of its frontages are creations of the past 30 years.'

The worst restriction on this route was the inadequate crossing of St Augustine's

Reach by the Drawbridge at the bottom of Clare Street. The term drawbridge was something of a misnomer, as this was actually a swing bridge that was opened whenever a vessel needed to pass. The Corporation eventually reacted to years of mounting public frustration with the delays and queues it caused, and in 1892 the upper section of St Augustine's Reach beyond the drawbridge was covered over and the narrow drawbridge was replaced by a wide fixed bridge – St Augustine's Bridge – which effectively marked the new entrance to the culverted river Frome. The usefulness of the dock beyond the drawbridge had lessened owing to the increasing size of ships but its removal was opposed by the Docks Committee and individuals like Ernest Lorymer, a corn merchant, who successfully sued for the loss of access by water to his premises. Nevertheless, the issue was an indication of the diminishing influence of the docks on city affairs and also of the strength of voice of road users several years in advance of the arrival of motor vehicle traffic.

In the half century after 1850 the Street Improvement Committee made many other modifications to city streets. Redcliff Street, which was described as 'a disgrace to the city', was widened in 1874. Other road improvements resulted in the loss of much old property: the aptly named Steep Street, for example, narrow and picturesque, with its run-down seventeenth-century houses, had once formed part of the main route north-west out of the city but was demolished in 1871. Fortunately, its picturesque appearance attracted the attention of artists and also of photographers such as John Hill Morgan, whose superb views are reproduced here. The Dutch House, an imposing timber-framed house on the corner of Wine Street and the High Street, only just survived demolition in 1908 on the casting vote of the Lord Mayor, although the ground floor was still cut back to widen the road. The new buildings, offices and factories, that took their place helped to change the face of the city; they brought a new style of architecture –robust façades of round arches and arcades in polychrome brick, loosely Italianate in inspiration and somewhat inappropriately termed 'Bristol Byzantine'. The building of several new factories also resulted in large scale clearance in the central area: Fry's, for example, were responsible for the demolition of much old property around the Pithay. Fortunately, Fry's made a photographic record before demolition of the old buildings. After 1850 some of the worst slums in the city were also cleared by the Sanitary Committee, and for all these reasons the population of the central area fell. By the 1880s the population of Bedminster was greater than than that of the inner city.

Victorian Bristol was widely considered to be one of the worst lit cities in England. In 1893 'Lesser Columbus' (Leonard Cohen) described Bristol as the 'worst lighted city' in the United Kingdom. Gas lamps had made their debut on Bristol streets in 1817, but in 1850 some parts of the city remained without lighting altogether. Those streets with lamps were still gloomy for the standards were generally set too far apart and the simple flat flame burners of the lamps emitted a poor light. In 1891 the

Corporation's Electrical Committee recommended lighting the central streets with electric arc lamps. On 20 November 1893 the first lamps were brought into use on Bristol Bridge and in nearby streets. With 1,000 candle-power lights supported on elegant, tall standards, they were an immediate success; in 1898 the lamps were extended to Whiteladies Road and Clifton, and by the early 1900s they were a familiar item of street furniture throughout the city and the suburbs.

Mid-nineteenth century Bristol was also one of the dirtiest and most unhealthy cities in England. A Parliamentary Report on the Sanitary Condition of Bristol carried out in 1845 had found appalling squalor, especially in some of the crowded courts and alleys occupied by the poor in the centre of the city. Overcrowding, low standards of cleanliness, contaminated water from old wells and pumps and inadequate drainage were found in Lewin's Mead, Temple and St Philips. Raw sewage emptied into the stagnant waters of the Floating Harbour and into the Frome, which was particularly filthy between St John's Bridge and Quay Head. Here, the ramshackle privies of old houses overhung the river and deposited sewage directly on to the river mud. The stench was intolerable, especially in warm weather, and the insanitary conditions contributed to several serious outbreaks of cholera and typhoid between the 1840s and 1860s. In 1849 a cholera epidemic in Bristol caused 444 deaths.

Following the 1848 Public Health Act, a Local Board of Health was established in 1851 to begin the process of cleaning the city. From 1855 main sewers were laid and home owners were obliged to make connections to them. The creation of a system of drains and sewers was a major Victorian achievement: an invisible but supremely important part of the city's modernisation – transforming living conditions and reducing the mortality rate substantially between 1850 and 1870. By 1874 there were 43 miles of sewers in place carrying the sewage to the tidal Avon below the Cumberland Basin. Foul cesspits and other nuisances were also removed, crowded and disease-ridden slums gradually demolished and refuse collecting and street cleaning improved. After 1847 homes began to receive piped water supplies from the Bristol Water Company and the old inadequate pumps and wells were removed. The results were dramatic: the death rate in Bristol fell from twenty-nine per thousand in 1845 to twenty by 1880, and in 1869 *The Times* described Bristol as one of the healthiest towns in Great Britain.

The Victorians reshaped Bristol in a slow and piecemeal process, but succeeded in preserving the dense cityscape that was only undone during and after the Second World War; nevertheless, much of Victorian Bristol remains with us now, testimony to the scale and permanence of their achievement.

Bristol Bridge from Welsh Back, 1850s. Bristol acquired its name in Saxon times from the bridge spanning the Avon here. The bridge marked the limit upstream accessible to sea-going ships and only barges and other small craft could continue eastwards to the expanding industrial suburbs of St Philip's Marsh and beyond. A medieval stone bridge of 1247 was replaced between 1764 and 1768 by this elegant three-arched and balustraded bridge designed by James Bridges; however, by the 1850s it was proving too narrow to cope with the expanding volume of road traffic between the centre and Temple Meads railway station. In 1861 the eastern side was widened by adding a cantilevered pavement supported on columns, resulting in the removal of the Portland stone balustrade and toll houses at each end. The remaining pair of toll houses were removed in 1873–4 when the west side of the bridge was widened. The boats in the foreground are tied up at Welsh Back and the factory chimneys in the background belong to Conrad Finzel's sugar refinery on Counterslip.

St Nicholas's church with Bristol Bridge in the foreground, between 1913 and 1920. The extra width to the bridge achieved by adding cantilevered pavements each side is clearly visible in this view as two Brislington-bound trams cross. The statue of Samuel Morley, a Liberal Member of Parliament for Bristol from 1868 to 1885, was erected beside St Nicholas's church in 1887 and moved to the Haymarket in 1921 to ease traffic congestion.

High Street, May 1858. The Druid Arms next to St Nicholas's church was demolished for the widening of Nicholas Street in 1864; the Angel Inn, next door, having lost its centuries-old neighbour, then collapsed! Seventeenth-century timber-framed gabled houses interspersed with Georgian buildings mainly of brick typified mid-nineteenth century Bristol streets: many were to go as the Victorians made their mark. (J.W.G. Gutch)

High Street, c. 1912. Insurance offices built in 1866 occupy the corner of Nicholas Street, while electric arc street lighting, overhead tram wires, a letter box, telephone sign and a monument to Liberalism (the Morley statue) all testify to Victorian progress.

The Dutch House, corner of Wine Street and High Street, *c*.1909. This was actually a Bristol merchant's house of about 1676. In 1908 a recommendation that it should be removed to widen the road was only defeated by the casting vote of the Lord Mayor. Instead, it was refurbished and the ground floor cut back to allow some road widening; the photograph was taken shortly after this was completed. The house remained a curiosity of Bristol until destroyed in the Blitz of 24 November 1940.

St Augustine's Reach, with a three-masted barque moored on the left alongside St Augustine's Parade, 1868. Bristol Quay along the channel of the Frome brought ocean-going merchant ships into the heart of the city, creating the forest of ships' masts amongst the streets which so impressed visitors. Fred Little captured this sight at about the time the docks entered a slow decline; the Floating Harbour could only accept the smaller types of steam-powered vessel so new, deep water docks were opened downstream at Avonmouth in 1877 and Portishead in 1879.

Welsh Back, c. 1875. The churches of All Saints, Christ Church, St Nicholas and, further right, St Mary-le-Port, and a chimney-stack belonging to J.S.Fry's, form a backdrop to sailing vessels berthed at Welsh Back on the left and at Redcliff Back, right. There are no steamships in the scene although a 'lighter' (a barge requiring towing), possibly laden with grain, might be going further up river. The covered sheds, warehouses and the impressive brick granary of Wait & James, corn and flour merchants, designed by Ponton & Gough in 1869 and seen on the left, are evidence of the industrialised aspect of this section of the Floating Harbour.

Broad Quay and the Drawbridge from St Augustine's Parade, *c.* 1875. The Drawbridge just visible on the left, built in 1868, was actually a swing bridge and was often the cause of congestion on this important route between Clifton and Temple Meads. In 1864 a survey of traffic showed that from 5 a.m. in the morning to 10 p.m. 30,318 passengers, 1,634 carriages, 1,382 carts and 130 horses crossed the bridge.

St Augustine's Bridge and the Tramway Centre, *c.* 1910. Until 1892 sea-going vessels entering St Augustine's Reach were able to go as far as Stone Bridge near Small Street, and road traffic had to cross by the narrow Drawbridge. In May 1893 a wider, fixed crossing – St Augustine's Bridge – was opened to relieve traffic congestion and the Frome was covered over beyond the new fixed crossing; thus, several years before the appearance of motor vehicles on Bristol's streets, the demands of road traffic predominated over those of dock users.

Tramway Centre, between 1908 and 1910. Following the covering over of the Frome beyond St Augustine's Bridge, gardens were laid out in Colston Avenue and the Tramways Centre established. The trams stopped alongside a triangular paved area overlooked by the offices of the Bristol Tramways & Carriage Company in the gabled building with its well-known clock, which was added in about 1900. Horse-drawn trams first ran on Bristol streets in 1875 and were an immediate success; however, they were slow and struggled against the city's many gradients – even with the aid of additional trace horses. Electric trams were introduced in 1895: they made light of the hills and by 1900 the horses had gone. The electric trams were effective shifters of people and were important in bringing the expanding suburbs within reach of the centre. In 1908 each day, from 5.30 in the morning to 11.30 at night, 1,666 trams left the Tramway Centre for the suburbs with a passenger capacity in excess of 99,000.

The BTCC was also the major provider of cabs and in 1908 introduced motor taxis, although the last horse cab was not withdrawn until 1910. Here a four wheel horse-drawn 'growler' is seen at the taxi rank in the foreground. An electric advertisement for Bovril surmounts the roof of Insall & Sons, St Augustine's Parade, leading portmanteau and trunk makers in the city since 1829.

The Tramway Centre from 'E' Shed, late 1890s. An unusual view of the tramway centre through the imposing gateway to 'E' Shed, a dockside shed designed by Edward Gabriel in 1894, which the port authorities decided should hide its utilitarian character behind an embellished façade facing the Tramway Centre and College Green.

Old Market, 1897 or 1898. A busy scene in this important city thoroughfare soon after the Bristol Tramways & Carriage Company first introduced electric trams on the route from Old Market to Kingswood in 1895. Old Market was the second largest transfer point with four tracks and ample reversing and crossing facilities. The tram in the centre, resplendent in the Company's dark blue and ivory white livery is heading towards Kingswood pulling former horse-drawn car 103, whilst car 127 (left) heading for Eastville is one of a batch of low height trams specially built to pass under the railway bridge in Fishponds Road. Streets on the tramway company's routes, as seen here, were transformed by the addition of the web of wires carried aloft on elegant poles.

Two horse-drawn bakers' vans are stopped alongside T. Snow & Sons, grocers, next to the exotic Moorish style façade of the White Hart Hotel; this provided access and doubtless many a quick drink for those on their way to the Empire Theatre of Varieties, which opened in 1893. Next door again is the ironmonger's and cutler's shop of John Rich, established in 1839.

Redcliff Hill looking towards St Mary Redcliffe, *c.* 1910. Edwardian Redcliff Hill was a bustling thoroughfare with electric trams linking the city with Bedminster. Graceful tram poles, different to those in Old Market, support the tram wires. A wide variety of shops and businesses lined the street, including a saddler, tinsmith, oil and colour man, refreshment rooms and public houses, food, clothes and chemists' shops.

Clare Street, *c.* 1910. The business centre of the city where many banks, insurance offices and solicitors were located. On the right the Yorkshire Insurance Company occupies offices above Glass & Co., tobacconists, whilst opposite the Sun Fire Office displays two large trademarks based on firemarks, which used to be attached to insured properties. Silk hat making was an important city trade located in the fashionable parts of the centre, and further down the street is the sign of Daniel Parsley, hat maker.

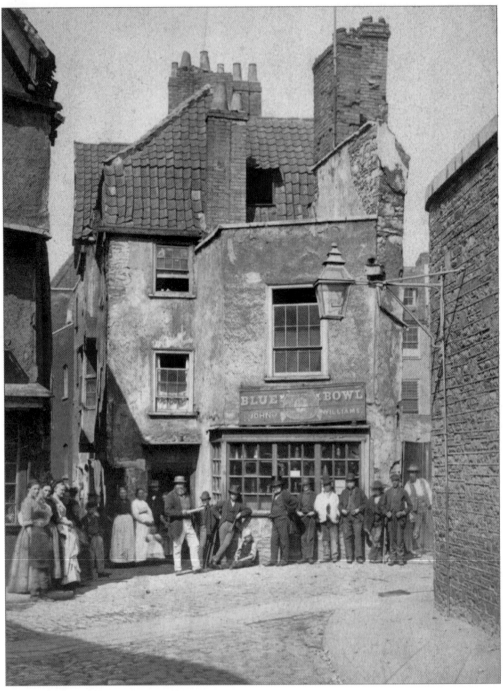

Blue Bowl Inn, Pithay, between 1870 and 1876. John Williams, whose name appears on the signboard, was the last landlord of the Blue Bowl Inn from 1870 to 1876, and this photograph from the Fry's company archive probably dates from 1876, shortly before it was pulled down to make way for Fry's number three factory. The man standing in front of the doorway is Thomas Denford, who worked for Fry's as an engine fitter (from 1869) and building works manager; he is holding some rolled paperwork – perhaps the drawings of the new factory – and may have been in charge of the demolition of the inn.

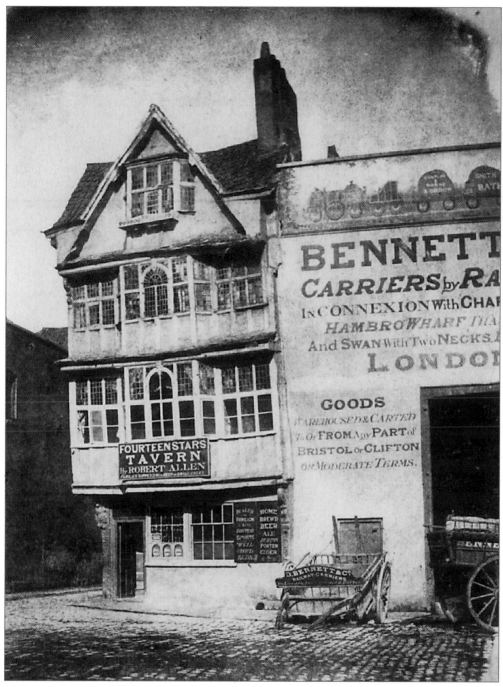

The Fourteen Stars Tavern, Counterslip, pre-1857. Carriers were usually located beside inns and here we see Bennett's warehouse making the most of its association with the modern steam railway and apparently dwarfing the Fourteen Stars, a frail survivor from the seventeenth century. Bennett began business in 1836 as a road carrier operating spring vans to London; by 1842 he was agent to the Great Western Railway 'forwarding to all stations on their line'. The tavern was demolished in 1857 to make way for Finzel's sugar refinery. (H. Owen)

Chapel Court, Pithay, between 1898 and 1902. A Dickensian scene of working men and boys standing amongst barrels of American crystal glucose, probably for use by Fry's in chocolate confectionery, in this cramped court enclosed by seventeenth- and eighteenth-century buildings soon to be swept away for the construction of Fry's factory number eight. The court took its name from the Baptist chapel of 1791, which is just visible on the extreme left and was used by Fry's in the late nineteenth century as a factory to make wooden boxes.

Bottom of Pithay, *c.*1880. The houses on the right recall Celia Fiennes's description of Bristol in 1698: 'The buildings of the town are pretty high, most of timber work, the streets are narrow and something darkish because the roomes on the upper storys are more jutting out.' The houses on the right were demolished to make way for Fry's factory number four in about 1880. The ground floor windows are boarded up and many window panes have been smashed.

The Frome under Union Street, 12 September 1871. Until the mid-nineteenth century the course of this river through the city was little more than an open sewer; the privies of old houses lining the river emptied directly into it causing a dreadful stench and spreading diseases such as cholera and typhoid. In stages, between 1857 and 1867, the course of the Frome through the city centre was covered over creating two new thoroughfares – Rupert Street and Fairfax Street – whilst the Board of Health Committee formed in 1851 started a major clean-up of the city, laying sewers, cleaning the streets and clearing the worst of the city's slums.

This photograph from the Fry's archive shows the recently culverted river by the Union Street bridge, one of thirteen that once spanned the river in the city. The man on the left is W. Clarke, a Fry's employee, and the man on the right is Thomas Denford who also worked for Fry's (see page 26). Denford's 'Time Books' for the early 1870s survive, and record that from late August until the week ending 13 September 1871 he had two labourers, H. Cox and W. Lovell, paving a yard and culvert: this is probably the work being carried out here. It is less clear why the fashionable Bristol photographer G. Guttenburg should record this fairly mundane job! Denford lived at 32 Victoria Street near Stapleton Road from the early 1870s and died in 1903 aged about seventy-three. (G. Guttenburg)

Leonard Lane, off Corn Street, 1850s. The worst slums were found in the centre in old properties like these, dating from the seventeenth century or earlier; most had been cleared by 1900. (John Bevan Hazard)

Houses in Narrow Weir, between 1887 and 1894. The weir was a tributary of the Frome and once diverted water to a mill in Castle Mill Street. J. Llewellin, firework maker, occupied premises here from 1887 to 1894; the building he occupied was demolished in the early 1900s.

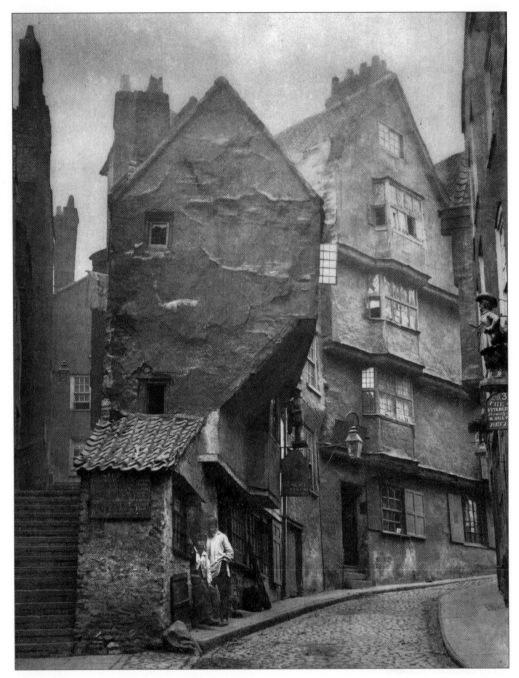

Steep Street, 1866. Until demolition by the City's Street Improvement Committee in 1871, travellers leaving the city for Gloucester and Wales via the Aust ferry had to climb the appropriately named Steep Street. In this view the signs of two chimney sweeps stare each other out across the street. (J.H. Morgan)

Steep Street from the junction with Trenchard Street (right) in 1866. These two views were photographed by John Hill Morgan of Parklands, Tyndalls Park, and published as a limited edition of 100 in 1891 by Frost & Read, 8 Clare Street and 47 Queens Road, Clifton. (J.H. Morgan)

All Saints Street, *c.* 1880. Backs of old houses soon to be demolished to make way for Fry's factory number four, completed in 1885. Joseph Storrs Fry (1826–1913) is seen fourth from left wearing a top hat and further right is Thomas Denford who also appears in the views on pages 26 and 30.

The Prince of Wales public house, Tower Lane, Pithay end, 1896 or 1897. According to the sign Alfred E. Gazzard was the landlord here – one of the many public houses owned by Georges & Co., the largest brewers in Bristol by the late nineteenth century. Their beers, ales and stouts are advertised prominently, while a poster in the window advertises a show at the Tivoli Palace, a tavern music hall in Broadmead which opened in 1870 as the Alhambra and closed in 1900. (T. Protheroe, Wine Street, Bristol)

The Royal Hotel, College Green, 1870s. The photograph was taken on a warm summer's evening; the sun is in the west and a man reads by an open window to the left of the hotel entrance. It probably dates to within a few years of the building of the hotel in the mid-1860s as the stonework looks very clean. The prospectus of the College Green Hotel Company was launched in October 1863 with a capital of £40,000 in £10 shares and the hotel opened in March 1868. In April 1871 the national census enumerators found the hotel contained a resident staff of over thirty, including a French cook, kitchen maids, scullery maids, housemaids, porters and even a billiard marker, waiting on seventy-one guests, amongst whom were an MP, a colonel, several barristers, bankers, north country manufacturers and a ship owner.

College Green, an old-established open space, was altered considerably after 1850. In that year a replica high cross was located at the apex of the lawn. In the mid-1860s part of a Georgian row of houses overlooking the green was demolished to make way for the hotel; to the right of the hotel a signboard is faintly visible below the window of one of the surviving Georgian houses advertising G.E. Lomas, an importer of foreign wines and West Indian pickles, preserves and arrowroot from 1844 to 1879. In the 1880s a larger, ornate gas lamp replaced the one seen here, whilst the cross was moved to the centre of the green to make way for the Jubilee statue of Queen Victoria, erected in 1888. The churchyard of St Augustine's church, just visible on the left, was cut back in 1894 to improve access to College Green from the central area. The hotel's stonework, meanwhile, gradually darkened in the grimy city atmosphere.

A roof-top view of Redcliffe Street from St Mary Redcliffe looking towards the centre, *c.* 1879. Beyond the shops and Fairbrother's Temperance Hotel in the foreground, warehouses, granaries and mills dominate the skyline although the spire of St Nicholas is just visible through the gloom. Glass cones on Redcliff Back and the masts of ships in the Floating Harbour add to the variety of the scene.

The leaning tower of Temple church rises behind the Shakespeare Inn of 1636 and other seventeenth- and eighteenth-century houses in Victoria Street in the 1870s. The gabled houses in the centre were subsequently demolished to make a through way to Church Lane.

Victoria Street, between 1874 and 1895. A horse and wagon loaded with barrels followed by a horse-drawn tram approach the camera in Victoria Street. Temple Meads, the main railway terminus, was situated well outside the old central area and only reached after a circuitous journey. In 1871 a new direct route was created by cutting a swathe through late medieval property between Bristol Bridge and the station. In the early 1870s the thoroughfare called – predictably enough – Victoria Street was filled with imposing shops and warehouses of polychrome brick in an Italianate style, generally known as 'Bristol Byzantine'. Sadly, many were lost during and after the Second World War and only a few remain, mostly in a very forlorn state. All those visible in this view, including W. Parnall & Co.'s shop fittings store on the right at 108 Victoria Street, have gone.

Neptune in Victoria Street, c. 1910. The statue of Neptune cast in lead by the Bristol founder Joseph Rendell was first erected in Temple Street in 1723 and moved on two further occasions, each time finding himself in the way of building or road alterations. His fourth move to the junction of Temple Street and Victoria Street took place in 1872; he remained here until relocated to his present resting place overlooking St Augustine's Reach in 1949.

Shops at Temple Gate, 1892. Nearest the camera is Amelia Mapstone's newsagent and confectioner's shop, covered in enamel signs and posters for local and national newspapers. Between this shop and the Terminus Tavern in the background are a boot and shoe maker, a hair cutting saloon, Charles Crocome's refreshment rooms and a tobacconist.

Approach to Temple Meads railway station with BCTC Blue Taxi, registration AE 1847 leaving the station, c. 1910. The joint railway station of the Great Western Railway and the Midland Railway was built between 1865 and 1878, replacing the original Brunel terminus of 1840 seen on the left.

TRADE & INDUSTRY

Writing of Bristol in 1893, 'Lesser Columbus' called the city the 'Universal Provider'. 'There is scarcely anything', he wrote, 'that is not made in Bristol.' The variety and range of trades and industries in Bristol was considerable: mid-nineteenth century Bristol trade directories list over 300 trades and manufactures. Many important British industries were present in the city: coal mining, iron founding, heavy engineering, pottery and glass making, chemical industries, brewing, food processing, tanning and leather trades, cotton and a variety of clothing trades. As the financial centre of the region, Bristol was an important centre for banking and there were, besides, a whole multitude of retail trades supplying household goods and services. Within this range there were enormous contrasts: between large companies mass producing goods such as soap and candles, paper bags, chocolates and cigarettes using machinery and hundreds of semi-skilled workers in modern factories; and smaller businesses, often working in old, cramped workshops, relying on a relatively small, highly skilled and specialised workforce. Many of the city's trades and industries were interdependent: thus stoneware and glass bottle makers supplied containers to local brewers and manufacturers of soda water, ginger beer and lemonade; various engineering concerns were closely associated; and the relationship between Mardons who made cigarette packets for W.D. & H.O. Wills was so close that when the Imperial Tobacco Company was set up in 1901 to consolidate the interests of British manufacturers against the American Tobacco Company, Mardons joined the following year. No single industry dominated, however, and whilst some older industries declined others grew to take their place.

The port was vital to Bristol industry. Imports predominated: bulky raw materials such as corn, tobacco, sugar cane, timber, tallow and vegetable oils unloaded in the docks supplied the many factories situated around the docks. West India merchants imported luxury goods such as tea, coffee and spices which were sold by grocers in the city. In 1850 the tonnage of coastal shipping was greater than overseas; this was to change, however; parity was reached in 1890 and by 1914 foreign imports far outstripped coastal tonnage. The docks also generated business for the shipbuilding yards and for other ancillary trades such as sail makers, anchor smiths, ships' joiners and carvers. Bristol had an established reputation for excellence in shipbuilding and the building of the *Great Britain* in 1843 indicated that Bristol shipbuilders were capable of building modern ships of iron; nevertheless, after the 1850s the industry lost ground as the demand increased for ships larger than the Floating Harbour could accommodate. The late nineteenth century saw the closure of many yards, and by 1919 only Charles Hill & Son's Albion yard remained of any importance.

Other old-established Bristol industries slowly disappeared from the mid-nineteenth century. Sugar refining had been important in the city since the seventeenth century but declined in the nineteenth century as the industry switched to London, Liverpool and Glasgow, where unloading charges were lower. When Conrad Finzel's large refinery on the Counterslip failed in 1881 large scale refining in the city came to an end, and all refining ceased in 1908. Glass and brass making were two other industries important in the eighteenth and early nineteenth centuries that declined after 1850. Coal production from the collieries at Bedminster, Ashton and Easton reached a peak of 500,000 tons in 1875, but a rapid decline then followed and most of the mines had gone by the mid-1920s.

The city's economy, nevertheless, showed adaptability and resilience in the face of the decline of some of the older industries; new industries developed to take their place and in the second half of the nineteenth century Bristol underwent steady, if unspectacular, growth and in various ways the industries contributed to the process of modernisation. The period was notable for the expansion and consolidation of several major firms. In brewing, for example, the industry came to be dominated by Georges & Co., a business dating from the late eighteenth century that bought up other brewers and hundreds of public houses. (By the 1920s Georges had more than 700 tied houses in the Bristol region.) The old breweries once taken over were closed and Georges premises in Bath Street were successively enlarged. Christopher Thomas & Sons came to dominate the manufacture of soap and candles, and whilst several small firms continued in business none could match their output; in the 1870s this amounted to about 8 per cent of the national total. The larger companies expanded mass production, using large labour forces on a scale previously unknown in the city. Several thousand women and girls were employed in tobacco and chocolate industries – particularly in jobs requiring sorting and packing. In 1883 the *Bristol Times and Mirror* reported that the Great Western Cotton Works at Barton Hill employed 1,200 women and girls – 75 per cent of the total. The newspaper described how at certain times of the day the neighbourhood was filled with 'women and girls with headgear consisting of shawls, mostly of a red and white plaid . . . converging to or diverging from the portals of the cotton factory'.

Mass production was also achieved through the use of machinery. Established in 1786, Wills became the largest tobacco company in Bristol, producing pipe tobacco, cigars and cigarettes from 1871. The success of Wills's Wild Woodbines, introduced in 1888, was only made possible after the company acquired the British patent of the American Bonsack cigarette making machine, which could produce 1,500 cigarettes in eight minutes – as many as a hand operative would make in a day. Similarly, the expansion of the stationery and packaging industry was accelerated once machinery was in place. Elisha Smith Robinson started business in 1844 making paper bags by hand, but soon turned to machinery which vastly increased production; the success was such that in 1876 the company built new premises in Victoria Street to house more machines.

New factory buildings helped change the face of the city. They were not insignificant prefabricated buildings best hidden out of town on trading estates, but impressive structures intended to enhance the city. Robinson's new building in Victoria Street, designed by W.B. Gingell, was a stately building worthy of its location overlooking Bristol Bridge. Christopher Thomas & Bros, the Bristol Wagon Works and W.D. & H.O. Wills and other companies also built ornate factories, which, with their domes and cupolas, Italianate arches and polychrome brickwork created the distinctive 'Bristol Byzantine' style. The new factories were invariably steam powered, and by 1900 the large number of tall factory chimneys on the skyline gave parts of Bristol the appearance of a northern mill town.

New industries brought new skills. Besides innovations in printing and packaging by Mardons and Robinsons, light engineering – particularly in the field of transport – grew during the second half of the nineteenth century. Locomotive building in Bristol, notwithstanding a temporary collapse during the recession of the late 1870s, developed with two companies, the Avonside Engineering Company and Pecketts, establishing a reputation for cheap, robust shunting engines. With their distinctive copper-capped chimneys and brass domes, these were prettier than most. Railway carriages and wagons built by the Bristol Wagon Works enjoyed a worldwide reputation, and in 1900 Bristol entered the motor vehicle industry. Within a few years Sir George White, director of the tramway company, had attached the city's name to aeroplane design.

Some industries greatly added to the whole fabric of city life. The gas industry contributed to a better lit city and from the 1880s started supplying gas cookers on cheap weekly rents. The newspapers catered for an increasingly literate public and provided a forum for the discussion of contemporary issues – many of the developments featured in this book were the subject of robust correspondence in local newspapers. Their surveys of local industries, obituaries of leading citizens and historical features – like the 'Bristol As It Was – And As It Is' series carried in the *Evening News* in 1908–9 – all helped to strengthen the feeling amongst ordinary citizens of being part of Bristol.

Industry in Victorian and Edwardian Bristol was characterised by a strong local identity; of all the major employers only the Great Western Railway was based outside the city. The others were Bristol companies led by local families whose members exerted a strong personal influence on their workplaces and employees. Joseph Storrs Fry (1826–1913) arrived at the company's works in his brougham every morning at ten minutes to nine and then at nine o'clock read to his employees from the Bible. Other company directors were known personally by their workforces, and when they died the whole city mourned. Many individual company heads sat on committees of the City Council and were closely involved in the municipal improvements to the city, and several were elected mayor. Mark Whitwill, Sir George White, the Frys, the Wills and other leading industrialists were heavily involved in good works, personally financing new educational, health and recreational amenities in the city; several were also deeply committed to missionary work amongst the poor. The contribution of local industrialists towards the modernisation of the city was thus far greater than the development alone of trade and industry.

View from St Mary Redcliffe looking over the Floating Harbour to Bristol Bridge, believed to have been taken in 1872 from the scaffolding erected to complete the spire. The industrial character of Victorian Redcliffe is clearly seen with several factory chimneys rising above the roof tops between the harbour and Redcliffe Street on the right. Vessels of various kinds crowd the quayside at Welsh Back. The massive bulk of Proctor Baker's granary and mill with its large, square chimney-stack dwarfs the neighbouring industrial premises on Redcliff Back. Opposite, across the harbour on Welsh Back, is the equally imposing granary belonging to Waite & James, designed by the Bristol architects Ponton & Gough in 1869.

View from St Mary Redcliff looking towards Temple Church in 1872. The view emphasises the densely packed townscape of the parishes of Redcliff, Temple and St Thomas south of the Avon. In the nineteenth century the area contained several important industries including corn mills, pottery and glass kilns, Wills's tobacco works and Robinson's printing and stationary business.

These parishes also contained a large working population. Behind the principal streets there were many crowded courts and alleyways where some of the worst slum conditions in the city existed. They were the homes of labourers and dock porters and others such as millers and potters employed in the local industries: in 1871 Hamilton Court, for example, off St Thomas Street, was inhabited by several labourers, a shoe-maker, a railway man, a painter, haulier and woollen draper's assistant. There were also basket-makers, harness-makers, wheelwrights, pipe-makers and many other small tradespeople living in the area, reflecting the diversity of commercial and industrial activity in Victorian Bristol.

Pottery cones on Temple Back are visible in the distance. St Thomas Street runs diagonally from the top left until it joins Phippen Street in the right foreground. Buildings in Portwall Street occupy the rest of the foreground and conspicuous bottom left is the Methodist Free Chapel built in 1859; next to it are the premises of Lucy Rowe, a forty-two-year-old widow in 1871, who, with the help of one assistant and a general servant, made a living as a rag dealer and bottle merchant – the roof of her bottle store can be clearly seen.

Redcliff Wharf, *c.* 1878. Redcliff Back was one of the oldest wharfs in Bristol, dating from the middle ages. *Lookout*, a three-masted barque of 216 tons gross with a wooden hull, 112 ft long, was built in Workington in 1858; this was a typical mid-Victorian vessel, characteristic of the ocean-going vessels found trading in the old harbour in the city in the third quarter of the nineteenth century. From 1869 to 1878 she belonged to Lucas Brothers, African merchants, who in 1878 owned eight other barques and a brig – a two-masted square rigger.

Lucas Brothers traded with West Africa, the source of palm oil used to make soap, ivory and cocoa. The family business was started by William Lucas in Marsh Street in about 1823. By 1851 the business was based at Bathurst Basin where it remained until about 1877, when operations were moved to Redcliff Wharf. This photograph dates from either the spring of 1877, when the ship was in port between voyages to the West Coast of Africa, or the summer of 1878 upon her return. Shortly afterwards she was sold to W.H. Williams of Newquay, Cornwall, and continued in use until about 1896. Lucas Brothers ceased trading in about 1907. Members of the family were active citizens serving on the Council and as Merchant Venturers. John Lucas, one of the partners, lived at Redland Bank, which is illustrated on page 84.

Behind the wharf on Redcliff Hill is the shot tower built by William Watts, a Redcliff plumber in 1782. Lead shot was first made here by Watts's patent which involved molten lead falling the height of the tower into a vat of a cold water where the droplets solidified. At the time of this view the works were owned by Sheldon Bush & Co., patent shot and lead pipe manufacturers. This well-known Bristol landmark was demolished for road widening in 1968.

Souvenir postcard of the opening of the Royal Edward Dock, opened by King Edward VII and Queen Alexandra on 9 July 1909. This new dock was constructed as a response to the ever increasing size of cargo steamers and consisted of a huge basin reached by a lock 875 ft long, large enough to take any vessel in existence. The opening was the occasion for lavish public demonstration of civic pride, which is reflected here on this postcard.

Albion ship yard, *c.* 1910. The terraced housing of Southville forms a backdrop to the Albion ship yard, the most important and long lasting in Bristol, although here there is little apparent activity on either the launching way on the right or in the dry dock. The yard was founded by the Hillhouse family and owned by Charles Hill & Sons from 1848. The clock tower of the main office dominates the view and the manager's house, covered in creeper, is visible further to the left.

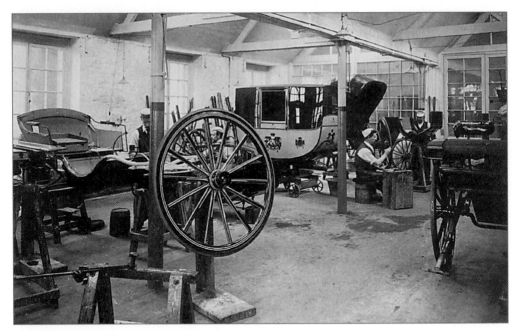

Coach painting loft of John Fuller & Co., St George's Road, *c.* 1910. Coach and carriage building was an important and old-established industry in Bristol. James Fuller took over Harper & Wolf's coach building business in 1815. The trade was highly skilled and specialised; the painting of carriages was a slow process with as many as eight or ten coats of paint and varnish applied, each one smoothed and polished before the next was added to achieve a durable and glossy finish.

Workforce of the Bristol Motor Company, Redcross Street, *c.* 1906. Bristol's first motor car was made in 1900 and the Bristol Motor Company was established by Arthur Johnson and William Appleton in 1902. The workshop equipment seen here powered by overhead line shafting includes a pillar drill, lathe and mechanical hacksaw.

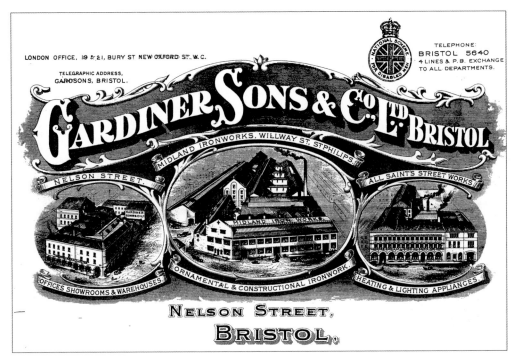

Bill-head of Gardiner Sons & Co., ironfounders and ironmongers, 1916. Entering business in 1860, Gardiners soon became leading wholesale and retail ironmongers in the city, supplying a wide range of fireplaces, kitchen equipment, sanitaryware and other domestic hardware besides manufacturing architectural iron and brasswork. The company remains in business today as a DIY and furnishings store.

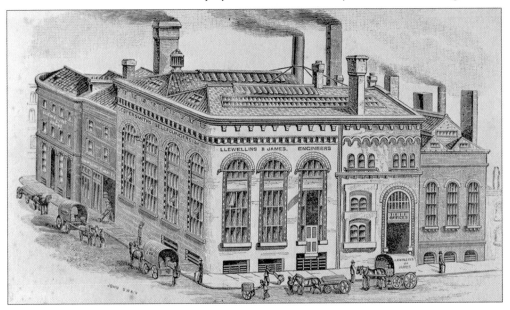

Llewellins & James brass foundry, Castle Green, 1889. There were several brass founders and coppersmiths in Bristol in the second half of the nineteenth century and Llewellins & James were by far the largest. In 1866 they employed about a hundred men and boys in the manufacture of bells, engineers' and plumbers' brassware, brewery equipment, gas light fittings and domestic copperware.

Fry's factories, between 1898 and 1902. New factories of J.S. Fry & Sons, chocolate manufacturers, in gleaming cream and red brick rise above old pantiled roofs in the Pithay. Fry's traced their foundation to 1728 and expanded dramatically after the 1850s to become one of the largest companies in Bristol. Number two factory, on the right, was built in 1860 and from then until 1914 a further ten factories were added to meet the expanding trade. Most of the works were situated in this cramped city centre location centred around the Pithay until 1923, when the company began the move to a new greenfield site at Somerdale, Keynsham. Number three factory is in the centre and number four, dated 1885, is on the left; factory bridges linked the individual blocks. Number three factory was demolished in 1937, number two the following year, but the left-hand chimney remained a city centre landmark until January 1961. (Lewis R. Protheroe, 3 Narrow Wine Street)

Girls counting and arranging chocolates in fancy boxes and bags at J.S. Fry & Sons, c.1908. As the popularity of eating-chocolate grew in the late nineteenth century, so the company's output rose and after 1885, Fry's produced more chocolates than cocoa. The number of Fry's employees rose from 193 in 1867 to 4,600 in 1908, including over 2,000 women and girls engaged mainly in wrapping and covering.

Cigar manufacture, W.D. & H.O. Wills, c.1912. Established in 1786, Wills became the largest tobacco company in Bristol producing pipe tobacco, cigars and, from 1871, cigarettes. Women are seen here working under electric arc lamps packing Rajah cigars; by 1901 Wills's workforce totalled 3,000. (Veal & Co.)

Laundry team,1890s. The exact location in this photograph is unknown, although it is believed to be a Bristol scene showing a group of laundry workers in a rather untidy backyard: the man on the left is holding a laundry stick, three women are holding newly starched collars, shirt fronts and bonnets whilst another three, wearing heavy aprons, are holding scrubbing brushes.

Telling Room, Capital & Counties Bank, c. 1895. This company opened its first Bristol branch in Victoria Street in 1878, moving to Clare Street in 1884. Amalgamation was an important trend in banks from the late nineteenth century and old-established Bristol banks such as Stuckeys disappeared in this period; the Capital & Counties Bank was taken over by Lloyds in 1918.

THE INDUSTRIAL SUBURBS

In 1850 nowhere in Bristol was far from the countryside: as late as 1874 two young boys playing near their home in St Pauls strayed as far as Horfield – then open countryside – and on a cold night Archie Walters, the elder of the two, died of exposure. Within twenty years rows of neat little terraced housing had completely transformed this scene, rapidly encroaching upon the Horfield countryside. In virtually every direction from the the centre, nurseries and farms were engulfed by new housing to accommodate Bristol's expanding population. By the early 1900s it was possible to travel for several miles from the centre before encountering open country. As in other cities, the new suburbs were socially differentiated with fashionable, residential suburbs in the west and areas of mainly working-class housing – the industrial suburbs – developing to the north, east and south.

Until the 1850s most of Bristol's working population lived in the old city, especially in St Philips, Redcliff and Temple where much industry was located; but as the old crowded courts and streets were converted to industrial and commercial use, the population of the inner city declined. Rows of small houses spread south in Bedminster and immediately east of the centre, stimulated by the arrival of the railway at Temple Meads. The opening of the Great Western Cotton mill was largely responsible for the suburban development of Barton Hill, and the growth of the collieries in Easton caused development there. St Philip's Marsh, an island between the Feeder Canal and the southward loop of the Avon, grew from the 1850s, creating a grid-iron of streets of red brick terraces, churches and chapels, corner shops and spit-and-sawdust public houses like the Victoria of 1873 – known affectionately to islanders as the 'Pig and Whistle'. In 1874 the Marsh was described as 'a gloomy vale enshrouded in almost perpetual smoke . . . home of the manure factories, bone crushing mills, knacker yards, horse flesh boiling factories and works in which the manufacture of chemical products throws off nauseous gases'. This was the archetypal industrial suburb with a working population tied closely to local industry: in 1871 Victoria Terrace in the Marsh (see page 124) was home to several labourers working in the neighbouring brickyards and potteries – including oven men and saggar makers; the terrace also housed a railway porter, a basket maker, a horse slaughterer and labourers working in the gas works and oil mills. The streets close to the engine sheds and Temple Meads station were full of engine drivers and other railway workers, whilst concentrations of coal miners were found in parts of Bedminster and Easton: in 1891 West Street in Bedminster, for example, had more colliers than any other occupation, although there were many general labourers and wives working as laundresses. Following the arrival of W.D. & H.O. Wills in Bedminster in 1886 many jobs were created in the area in the tobacco industry, and between 1851 and 1901 the population of Bedminster rose from 19,424 to 70,107.

Most of the housing consisted of terraced rows. Although no longer fashionable, the terrace remained the speculative builder's answer to the demand for cheap urban housing until the early 1900s. Cheap on land, materials and largely devoid of ornament, those built until the late 1870s were usually plain fronted with a parapet hiding a low roof supported against an extension of the party walls, which saved on roof timber. All Bristol's terraces were through houses with a rear back yard; there were no back-to-backs as in many northern towns, but the smaller house often lacked a through hall and opened straight on to the pavement. A superior plan incorporated a two-storey extension at the rear which provided space for a back kitchen, WC and coal shed as well as more bedroom space. The better quality house had a through passage which, in imitation of larger houses, promoted greater differentiation of room use: the front parlour was usually kept for best – a room for show facing the street – whilst the family lived in the back room or 'kitchen', separate from the back kitchen which housed the cooking range and washing copper.

As the suburbs grew they acquired their own distinctive character. The rows of terraced houses were followed by churches and chapels: new parishes were created – often supported by substantial middle-class aid to further religion amongst the labouring classes and help improve standards of moral behaviour. St Silas's, a new parish church for St Philip's Marsh, on the Feeder Road, was consecrated in 1867, and others followed in Bedminster and in the eastern suburbs. Many Nonconformist chapels were also built and by the early 1900s there were several Salvation Army and YMCA halls in the poorer districts. All the religious organisations aimed to reduce drunkenness amongst the working classes. In the mid-nineteenth century beer was the drink of working men and public houses were an important part of the working-class environment. John Latimer, the Bristol historian, reckoned that the number of inns, taverns and beer shops in the whole of Bristol rose from 650 in 1840 to about 1,250 in 1870, and the majority were to be found either in the old city or in the industrial suburbs. Some were named after local industries: the Mechanics Arms, for example, the Forgeman's Arms and the Colliery Tavern. However, writing in

1887, John Latimer remarked on the improved 'social habits' of the working classes since the mid-nineteenth century. The temperance movements and the churches may have had some success in reducing alcohol consumption; certainly the example of James Cox on page 102 is a striking story of the conversion of one rough, hard drinking individual with the help of the local Wesleyan chapel. The operation of the Licensing Act of 1872 fixed the closing time on Sundays at ten o'clock and was also instrumental in reducing the excessive number of beer shops, which had been able to obtain a licence at little cost. New leisure pursuits which developed towards the end of the nineteenth century also provided attractive alternatives to the public house. Nevertheless, public houses remained an integral part of social life in the industrial suburbs into the twenty-first century, and in 1910 there were some thirty-three public houses in Bedminster alone.

The main thoroughfares, for example East Street, Bedminster, became important local shopping centres. Grocers' shops – frequently licensed to sell alcohol – grew rapidly in the late nineteenth century, often occupying a street corner amongst the rows of terraces; by the early 1900s there were also some twenty grocers' shops belonging to the Bristol Co-operative Society, founded in 1884. Fried fish shops became another distinguishing feature of the working-class districts in the late nineteenth century providing cheap nutritional food. In 1905, the first year they were listed separately in local directories, there were seventy-four fried fish dealers in Bristol, all located in the poorer districts, and five years later their number had increased to 126.

Other facilities were gradually added to the industrial suburbs. Schools were provided by the School Board established by the 1870 Education Act, and following the 1874 Public Libraries Act branch libraries were soon established in St Philips and Bedminster. Parks were created providing space for sport and leisure. The industrial suburbs, in effect, became self-contained communities. Bedminster, in particular, saw itself as a town within a city, a place apart, which by the time of the First World War was important enough to have its own music halls and cinemas.

The tramway was another essential part of Bristol's industrial suburbs from 1875 and stimulated development further afield. Before the advent of trams the areas of working-class housing were still close to the centre, but once tramlines were laid on major routes out of the city large-scale urban development began in Horfield, Bishopston, Eastville, Stapleton and Fishponds. Building was delayed by a slump in the early 1880s, but resumed before the end of the decade and continued at a furious pace through the 1890s, a decade which also saw extensive development south of the Avon in St Annes, Totterdown, Southville and in the new suburb growing up around the docks at Avonmouth.

The terraces of this second major phase of development are easily distinguished from those built before 1880. The most striking difference is in the façade, which frequently incorporates a bay window, either one or two storey, whilst the roof is integrated into the overall design projecting on eaves and pitched more steeply instead of being hidden behind a low parapet. There were many subtle variations in the size and quality of the terrace, and whilst these were evident before 1880 they became more pronounced from the late 1880s. The quality of the front elevation and also of the internal decorations – the amount of moulded plasterwork, joinery and the quality of the fireplaces – expressed the social hierarchy within the working class between the higher paid artisans and the unskilled labourer. And although Bishopston, Horfield, Southville and other areas may have lacked the exclusiveness of the affluent suburbs, they began to acquire a residential character of their own. By 1900 the distinction between the industrial and fashionable suburbs was less precise than it had been in 1875. Whilst the terraced houses built at the end of the nineteenth century may have been monotonous they were controlled by housing by-laws, which ensured that basic standards of construction, sanitation and adequate space, front and back, were maintained. The larger houses were villas within a terrace – many had names following the fashions of the affluent suburbs – and with their solid, respectable exteriors provided homes worthy of the upwardly mobile artisan class.

William Bailey, haulier, Feeder Road, St Philip's Marsh, between 1904 and 1909. The Stone Manure Company, horse slaughterers and manure manufacturers from 1888, was at the top of Arthur Street (left) on the Feeder Road. The company belonged to Arthur Stone who built twelve houses in Arthur Street in 1896–7. William Bailey, who is presumably seen standing here by his wagon, is recorded as a haulier in Feeder Road from 1904 to 1909.

Children pose for the camera outside Parker's corner shop, St Philip's Marsh, *c.* 1906. One or two are poorly dressed with open-toed shoes and ill-fitting clothes, but most appear to be wearing their best – the boys in Eton collars and one little boy on the right in a sailor's top; possibly the occasion was an outing to Weston-super-Mare.

Frederick Parker ran this shop on the corner of Short Street and Victoria Terrace between 1895 and 1910. Corner shops were an important part of working-class suburbs and provided for most of the regular needs of the local population. They were stocked with a wide range of goods usually mixed in glorious disarray, like the exterior advertisements here which mix foodstuffs and hardware: condensed milk – a cheap alternative to fresh milk was first introduced in the 1860s and the Swiss company Nestlé founded in 1904; cocoa and chocolate were no longer luxury goods and Fry's like the other major producers made cheap products within reach of the working-class family; a tin of Peak Frean's biscuits can also be glimpsed inside the door; Parker was also licensed to sell tobacco. Corner shops also supplied a wide range of hardware including soap (Hudson's were a Midlands firm), starch, laundry blue, candles, matches and black-lead; here we see Henkel's bleach advertised in the doorway and boxes of Lions black-lead used to polish grates and the kitchen range piled high inside the shop window.

St Philip's Marsh was a close-knit community broken up in the 1950s when the housing was cleared to make way for an industrial estate. Today, the site of the corner shop is an untidy scrap of wasteland bounded by barbed wire.

Upton Road, Southville, *c.* 1915. Many of the houses in this road were built between 1896 and 1898 but were overshadowed by Wills's factory number eight in Raleigh Road, which was originally used to pack tinned tobacco and snuff.

East Street, Bedminster, *c.* 1912. This busy shopping street is dominated by the imposing Gothic-style factory of W.D. & H.O. Wills, built of deep red Cattybrook bricks in 1886 and designed by Sir Frank Wills. The covered cart outside the factory belongs to Mardon Son & Hall, printers and packagers who had joined Wills in the Imperial Tobacco Group in 1902.

Corner of Brook Street and St John's Road, Bedminster, *c*.1919. A scene reminiscent of an urban landscape by the painter L.S. Lowry as workers – mainly women – emerge from the Wills factory on St John's Road. Most seem unaware of the photographer although some of the children have seen him, such as the girl in the centre foreground shading her eyes from the bright midday sun as she faces the camera. Her left shoe is open toed.

The close proximity of terraced houses and corner shop to the tobacco factory typify the environment of the industrial suburbs. The houses with their plain fronts and parapet roofs date from the 1870s and are typical of those built in the third quarter of the nineteenth century. The lantern of the gas lamp on the left has been painted blue – a First World War air raid precaution, introduced in March 1915, although there were no attacks on Bristol from German aircraft. The taller block on the right was a bonded warehouse built for the Imperial Tobacco Company by Cowlins in 1914. All the buildings on the right have now gone and the site is now occupied by an Asda supermarket; however, the shop on the corner survives.

St Luke's Road, Bedminster, *c*. 1910. This road bounding Victoria Park was developed from the late 1860s and through the 1870s with plain fronted terraced houses of a type common throughout Bristol's industrial suburbs.

George King and family outside their Bedminster home, 131 Whitehouse Lane, *c*. 1910. This plain brick terraced house which backed on to the railway line from Temple Meads was one of thirty-two houses erected by a builder called Adams in 1896; they were extremely small and basic with a parlour, kitchen and tiny scullery crammed into the main block, three small bedrooms upstairs but no rear extension, except for a small structure housing the WC.

Nutgrove Avenue, Victoria Park, Bedminster, *c.* 1910. In contrast to George King's small dwelling, opposite below, in Whitehouse Lane, just across the main railway line and Victoria Park were these substantial terraced houses in Nutgrove Avenue, also built in about 1896.

Victoria Park, *c.* 1910. In 1888 land at Windmill Hill, Bedminster, was purchased from Sir Greville Smyth and 51 acres were turned into a public park. Like many Victorian public parks it had a bandstand and a popular feature – a redundant cannon, this one a rifled muzzle loading gun probably dating from the 1870s. The industrial setting of the park is emphasised by the chimneys of Wills's factories in the background.

Badminton Road, St Agnes, *c.* 1910. Substantial terraced houses with two-storey bays in Badminton Road built in the mid-1890s belie the reputation of this district for poverty; Clifton College supported a mission here. The tower of St Agnes's parish church, consecrated in 1886, can be seen in the background.

Committee of the Loyal St George Sick Benefit Society, 1903. Voluntary associations such as this were common in working-class communities before the emergence of the welfare state. Standing from left: C.A. Broome, J. Walker, G. Johns, H. Stokes, T. Calloway, R. Dempsey, H. Mann, E. Mayo; seated: H.J. Silcocks, P. McCarthy, C.J. Strawbridge, D. Daley; front: R. Pearse, W.J. Headford, G. Thompson.

Maple Road, Horfield, *c.* 1894. Builders take a break from building a terraced row in Maple Road beween Thornleigh Road and Ash Road. The roofs are on but some wooden scaffolding remains and the joiner is still required to fit the sash windows and doors, and there is plenty of work for the plasterers seen here. The man standing confidently in the centre and the only one wearing collar and tie may be Walter Collison, the builder and contractor who submitted the plans for these houses to the Horfield Local Board (responsible for imposing statutory building regulations) on 19 April 1894.

Between 1892 and 1894 Collison, of 8 Church Road, Horfield, was responsible for the construction of some forty-eight terraced houses at the Gloucester Road end of Maple Road and a large number of similar houses in Thornleigh Road, Ash Road and Elm Road. A 'for sale' sign is visible in the photograph and Collison, who, like most small builders had probably taken out a loan to finance the speculation, was no doubt counting on a speedy sale. The houses were often bought by shopkeepers and other small tradesmen who let them out to tenants.

Collison's houses followed a typical plan, with a parlour and living room on the ground floor and a kitchen, coal shed and WC in a rear extension; upstairs there were three bedrooms but no bathroom. His houses had attractive façades of blue-grey Pennant sandstone and ashlar window and door surrounds. The bays had projecting roofs surmounted by terracotta finials. Sadly, many of the houses have been altered and have lost some of their original features, but they survive over a hundred years later and provide roomier and more attractive accommodation than much twenty-first century mass housing.

New Bridge, Ashton Gate, Bristol.

Ashton swing bridge, *c.* 1910. Opened in 1906, this bridge spanning the New Cut was a complicated and expensive structure: it was both a road and railway bridge and also a swing bridge which could open to allow tall masted vessels to pass. Operations were controlled from a cabin erected over the bridge.

The Round House Ashton Gate, Bristol.

Ashton Gate Toll House, Ashton Gate, *c.* 1910. This was one of fifteen turnpike gates in Bristol in the 1850s; the turnpike trustees levied tolls from road users to maintain the road. The last of the turnpikes was removed in 1867 and the roads came under municipal control. Most of the toll houses were demolished but this one survived and gave its name to the district, and, of course, a well-known football ground!

Timber trolley of Frederick Niblett, hauliers of 42 Parson Street from about 1909 to 1923, outside the White Horse, West Street, Bedminster, *c.* 1910. The empty timber trolley may be returning to Parson Street having off-loaded a delivery of timber to one of the timber dealers and saw mills then in business further up West Street. The driver is Tom Reeves, who is wearing clogs, gaiters and a woollen jersey under his jacket. Tram lines cross the foreground of the cobbled street, which shows signs of horse droppings, a common sight on roads when horses were the main source of motive power.

Public houses were an essential part of the working-class suburb; the White Horse, one of several pubs along West Street, was an old-established public house, listed in Mathews 1793–4 Bristol Directory. It was clearly given a major rebuild in the early 1900s. Advertisements for whiskies and port are displayed in the window and hanging by the entrance is a sign of the National Telephone Company, which provided by far the majority of Britain's telephones and exchanges from 1880 until 1911 when the GPO took over the entire telephone network. The outward appearance of the pub is little changed today.

Chessel Street on the right was developed between about 1899 and 1903, and contains typical small terraced houses of the period.

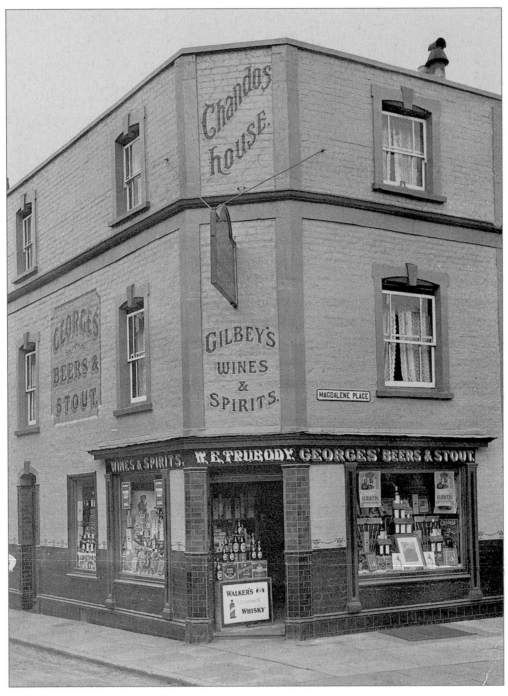

William Ernest Trubody's corner shop, 64 Magdelene Place, Lower Ashley Road, *c.* 1910. An attractive shop exterior with painted brickwork, a decorative frieze, tiles (probably dark green) around the door and shaded signwriting above for W.E. Trubody, grocer licensed to sell alcoholic beverages. Georges beers are also prominently advertised and some bottled beers can be seen displayed in the doorway. In 1850 there were 279 grocers and tea dealers in Bristol; by 1906, when Trubody entered business, the figure had risen to 881 including the co-operative shops. Trubody ran the shop until 1939.

Mr Brown's shop, Easton, *c.* 1905. The interior of a grocer's shop with typical fittings of the time: a long straight wooden counter and hanging shelves which are stacked with different varieties of Peak Frean's 'celebrated biscuits' and a box of Fry's chocolate creams. The gas light above the counter consists of simple flat flame burners which did not require glass chimneys or shades (see also the kitchen on page 115).

The industrial suburbs, east: Bath Road looking towards Brislington, *c.* 1910. Between the houses lining Bath Street, terraced houses of the 1890s in Upper Street, Totterdown, hang precariously from their steep hillside site above the Turnpike Inn, formerly the toll house on the turnpike road to Bath.

The industrial suburbs, west: Shirehampton station, *c.* 1912. The area west of the city was mainly associated with the affluent suburbs but Bristol acquired a small industrial suburb further west when Shirehampton and Avonmouth became part of Bristol, following the extension of the city boundaries in 1904. The railway opened in 1865.

THE FASHIONABLE SUBURBS

As working-class suburbs spread into the fields south and east of the old city, wealthy solicitors, accountants, mortgage brokers, insurance agents, doctors, merchants and manufacturers established their homes in Clifton, Cotham and Redland, and further afield in Sneyd Park, Stoke Bishop and Leigh Woods. There were exceptions: Knowle enjoyed a brief spell as a desirable area, there were some middle-class villas in Bedminster and enclaves of working-class terraced housing could be found in the affluent suburbs. Nevertheless, the general picture remains of quiet suburbs of substantial houses, an environment that embodied middle-class values and aspirations.

The fashionable suburbs represented the complete separation of work and home. In the eighteenth century industrialists and tradesmen usually lived over their working premises, but from the early nineteenth century affluent citizens withdrew from the city to Kingsdown and to Clifton. Secure from the noise, dirt and immorality of city life, the rising middle classes could lead respectable lives in their well-built villas in leafy roads with respectable names. And the road names were important, as they helped to create the right atmosphere: 'street' was not acceptable – it conveyed too much of the city; and in Clifton Gallows Acre Lane was renamed Pembroke Road. Lanes, after all, were rural, muddy and inconvenient and public executions were (from the 1860s) a thing of the past.

House names were important too: Albion, Richmond and Belmont Villa were solid and respectable and added to the uniqueness of the family home. Until the mid-nineteenth century the fashionable home in Bristol was typically within a terrace where the individual dwelling was subsumed within the identity of the whole block. They usually occupied commanding sites close to the street, square or pavement, and were public and very showy. The Victorian middle classes, in contrast, desired separateness and seclusion, and so from the mid-nineteenth century the fashionable terrace fell from favour and was replaced by the large detached or semi-detached villa. These were usually set back from the road offering greater privacy, and for the first time gardens became an important part of the urban home environment.

Separateness and individuality were also achieved through the style of the house. There were different styles to choose from: Grecian, Gothic and Tudor, but most popular was the Italianate style which was adopted for many large houses built in the 1860s. Typically, the large Victorian villa boasted large bay windows which not only added to the light and spaciousness of the interior but emphasised the importance of the window in the façade. Details could vary: window openings of carved Bath stone or moulded terracotta provided points of individual interest to each house. Gabled roofs were also popular and again decorative barge boards provided opportunities for individual treatment. Some of the houses were faced in ashlar like the detached houses in Victoria Square, Clifton, whilst others were rendered; but the finest and largest in parts of Clifton, Redland and Sneyd Park were built of grey or pink Pennant sandstone, which contrasted well with the light coloured Bath stone used for corners, door and window surrounds.

These houses were large – twelve rooms or more; families were generally larger but space was also required for the servants. Keeping servants was the distinguishing feature of being middle class: some of the grandest establishments in Royal York Crescent had as many as six including a butler; two servants – a cook and a parlour maid – was common; and in 1881 a modest row of houses in Auburn Road, Redland (the homes of a retired ship master, a commercial clerk, a minister, a solicitor's clerk and three young unmarried sisters), each had one resident female servant. The principal rooms of the house were usually situated over a basement which contained a suite of service rooms, separate, physically and socially, from the family areas. Plans of 1862 for villas in Tyndalls Park show stairs leading to a basement kitchen, scullery, wine cellar, pantry and house keeper's room.

The presence of servants and people in supporting trades – laundresses, dressmakers and shopkeepers – could account for a considerable percentage of the residents in an affluent suburb. In his study of Clifton, Donald Jones has shown that of a random sample of 709 houses over 47 per cent of the population comprised servants and others in service industries. Nevertheless, their presence did not affect the exclusiveness of the fashionable suburbs. In 1878 one Cliftonian could write to the *Bristol Mercury*, 'Poor people do not walk about on Clifton streets', adding, 'We have nothing common or unclean amongst us'. He and others wanted to keep it that way and objected strongly to the proposal to extend the 'disgusting tramway' into Clifton. The tram, they believed, threatened to bring the 'nasty, low inhabitants of Bristol' up into Clifton where they would encourage jerry building, depress property values and tempt residents to shop in Bristol to the detriment of local traders.

The extension to the tramway was, indeed, rejected by the City Corporation and Clifton remained free from the threat of lower-class immigrants. Clifton, however, was never a typical middle-class suburb; it owed its rise as a fashionable area to the nearby Hotwells, which had attracted wealthy people seeking a cure from the Hotwell water since the seventeenth century. Hotwells enjoyed its heyday in the mid-eighteenth century, but its popularity was already waning in the 1790s when speculative builders began the construction of large terraces overlooking the Gorge. From the heights above the Avon the residents of Clifton enjoyed life in an exclusive suburb with fresh air, clean water and pleasant views over to Somerset. Clifton always remained a place apart – even following its absorption into Bristol in 1835. There were stately terraces with graceful iron verandas, expensive shops in elegant streets, beautiful churches, public schools and good hotels, but no red brick public houses, no fried fish shops, few corner shops – and no trams. There was a strong upper middle-class, even aristocratic, air to Clifton; it was home to members of the gentry, senior Anglican Clergy, admirals, army officers, professional and literary people and, according to 'Lesser Columbus' in 1893, 'Unmarried ladies of matured, single experience'.

Clifton, Cotham and Redland grew rapidly after 1850 fuelled by the optimism of speculative builders. Within a year of the opening of the Clifton Suspension Bridge to road traffic in 1865 building lots were being advertised in Leigh Woods, and in the 1870s Alpenfels, the Swiss chalet-style house was built near the bridge for Francis Fox, the Chief Engineer of the Bristol and Exeter Railway. The expansion of Redland proceeded at a dramatic pace; in 1867 it was reported that 300 houses were being built in one scheme alone. From the 1870s the development crossed the Downs – secured as a public park by Act of Parliament in 1862 – to Sneyd Park and Stoke Bishop and, from the 1890s, Henleaze. The search for the fashionable home was taking the affluent Bristolian ever further from the old city.

Hotwells, 1850s. The old Hotwell house, dating from about 1696, was removed in 1822 to allow the construction of Bridge Valley Road. A new pump room was constructed, but this did not stop the decline of the spring and it was demolished when Hotwell Point was removed in 1868.

Hotwells pump, *c.* 1880. Following the removal of Hotwell Point on the Avon to improve navigation in 1868, the hot spring at the Hotwell was lost, and following local complaints this ornate pump was erected in 1877 within a cavern in the nearby cliff; however, it was doubted if this supplied the true spring water, and even if it did the distance between the source and the pump caused the water to lose its characteristic temperature.

Clifton Suspension Bridge, 1850s. For some ten years the famous suspension bridge designed by Isambard Kingdom Brunel (1806–59) lay abandoned. The two piers stood forlorn and unloved – they were considered an eyesore – and the Clifton Improvement Society even proposed their demolition! Work had begun in 1831 on the Clifton side, but it was the construction of the massive abutment on the Somerset bank which exhausted the funds, and work was abandoned in 1853.

Clifton Suspension Bridge, 1875. A new company was formed to complete the bridge in 1861 and work resumed the following year. The bridge was finally opened amidst huge celebrations on 8 December 1864. Brunel, however, did not live to witness the event: he had died in 1859 and never saw completed what is generally regarded as his masterpiece. The bridge was opened to vehicular traffic on 23 January 1865 and almost immediately stimulated the development of Leigh Woods on the Somerset side as an exclusive suburb.

Sion Hill, Clifton, 1870s. Elegant houses with first-floor iron balconies, typical of late Georgian Clifton, overlook the Avon Gorge and exude the air of a Regency seaside town. The St Vincent's Rock Hotel in the foreground was opened in October 1868 in the former pump room of the Sion spring, established in 1811; by 1845 the spring was also supplying piped water to 304 dwellings in the neighbourhood.

Grand Spa Hotel, Clifton, *c.* 1910. Typical late Victorian street furniture in Sion Hill includes, on the right, a cabman's rest, introduced in Bristol in 1874; an electric arc street lamp, introduced in Clifton from 1898; and a letter box, first appearing in Bristol in 1856: by 1908 there were 461. This one dates from 1879–87, and survives in 1996. The hotel was opened in March 1898 in a final attempt to re-establish the Hotwell.

The Royal Parade, Queens Road, Clifton, 1870s. A commercial terrace containing fashionable shops, designed by Foster & Wood in the 1850s.

George V visiting the Victoria Assembly Rooms, 1913. Designed by Charles Dyer and built in 1839–41, this impressive Grecian building served as a concert hall and meetings room for Clifton. George V unveiled the bronze statue of his father, Edward VII, by Henry Poole, surrounded by fountains on 4 July 1913. Here the King is seen saluting the crowd, which includes several women holding umbrellas to ward off the sun.

Regent Street, *c.* 1915. This was the main Victorian shopping street of Clifton. The W.H. Smith shop in Regent Street, opened in 1905, was the first in Bristol outside Temple Meads station.

Whiteladies Road, *c.* 1910. Whiteladies Road was subject to various street improvements in the second half of the nineteenth century, including road widening and better drainage. The tram lines were laid in 1874 and opened as far as Black Boy Hill on 9 August 1875; an extension to Westbury-on-Trym was opened on 23 October 1908.

Albert Hallet, confectioner, Black Boy Hill, Redland, 1899. Advertisements for Fry's chocolates adorn the windows of this shop, which was in business here from about 1878 until about 1917.

Vyvyan Terrace, Clifton, *c.* 1910. Named after Sir Richard Vyvyan (1800–79), a Conservative Member of Parliament for Bristol in the 1830s, this impressive Ionic-pillared terrace was built in the early 1840s and included the homes of members of Bristol's social elite throughout the rest of the nineteenth century.

Royal Promenade, Victoria Square, Clifton, *c.* 1910. Begun in the 1830s, Victoria Square contains some of the finest large terraces in Clifton, and this view shows Royal Promenade – a palatial group of fifteen houses designed by James Foster & Son in 1837 but not completed until the early 1850s. The square was not finished until 1874 by which time the popularity of the fashionable terraced house had waned.

Victoria Square, Clifton, 1850s. A magnificent four lantern gas lamp dominates the north-east side of the square; a similar lamp stood by the Victoria Assembly Rooms but these were exceptional: Bristol was one of the worst lit cities in the country in 1850. The effectiveness of this lamp would have been limited by mid-Victorian gas technology – the simple flat flame burners produced a poor light. Lansdown Terrace, built in 1835, is to the right, Royal Promenade in the distance.

Upper Belgrave Road, Durdham Down, *c.* 1910. These large Italianate villas are typical of those built in Clifton from the 1850s to replace the large terrace as the fashionable home for the affluent residents in Clifton, Cotham and Redland. Joseph Storrs Fry lived at number 16 until his death in 1913.

Roseneath, 6 West Park, Cotham, *c.* 1910. This was the home of Andrew and Frances Brewer and their children (see page 82), and is typical of the villa homes built in Clifton, Cotham and Redland in the third quarter of the nineteenth century. (A. Brewer)

View across the back gardens of houses in Rockleaze, Sneyd Park, *c.* 1875. Gardens became an important part of the Victorian middle-class suburb.

Ivywell Road, Sneyd Park, *c.* 1912. These substantial stone villas of the 1870s, each one clearly different from its neighbour, are set back from the road.

John Herbert Brewer (born 8 January 1913) with his monthly nurse, who stayed with the mother and child for one month after the baby's birth at 6 West Park, Cotham. His parents were Andrew Brewer (1870–1935), an accountant who worked in Bath, and Frances Edith Brewer (1870–1931). (A. Brewer)

Frances Harriet (born 1900) and Dorothy Edith (born 1902) on a toy horse in the back garden of 6 West Park, Cotham, c. 1906. (A.Brewer)

An Edwardian doll party at 6 West Park, Cotham, *c.* 1910. (A. Brewer)

Redland Bank, Redland Hill, *c.* 1875. This was home to John Lucas and his son Charles, African merchants; in 1871 four daughters were also resident and there were two servants, a domestic cook and a parlour maid. The house was demolished in 1961.

Maidservant laundering clothes, Redland Villa, home of the Feddon family, *c.* 1858. The servant population of the fashionable suburbs formed a substantial percentage of the total. In this carefully arranged composition the girl is posed scrubbing the clothes in a wooden wash tub – washing machines were virtually unknown in the 1850s. A hot water can sits in the foreground.

A HOME IN THE COUNTRY

Wealthy Bristolians had been moving out of the congested and polluted city for a quieter, more spacious country home since the eighteenth century, and the large houses in the countryside surrounding the city were a mix of the homes of rural landowners (the gentry), like the Sampsons of Henbury Manor, and those of wealthy Bristol industrialists. The Harfords, Bristol bankers and industrialists, had moved to the Blaise Castle Estate, Henbury, in 1789. Charles Thomas, soap and candle maker, whose factory poured smoke into the sky above Broad Plain lived in the peaceful surroundings of Pitch and Pay Lane in Stoke Bishop. The Grove, a late eighteenth-century house set in extensive grounds at Brislington, was the home of the Ricketts family, Bristol glass manufacturers until 1862; from 1878 until 1899 it was occupied by Richard Cripps, an importer of Italian marble at Redcliff Wharf. After 1900 urbanisation encroached upon Brislington and the house lost its rural character. The search for a home firmly in the country could take affluent Bristolians even further from the city. Lord Winterstoke (W.H. Wills) acquired a country estate at Blagdon, Somerset, where he assumed the identity of a typical large country landowner, developing a model farm and dairy.

Gentlemen landowners like the Sampsons in Henbury – the local squires – were owners of farms which were held on fixed terms by tenant farmers. There were many farms, smallholdings and market gardens around Bristol. There were sixteen farms alone in Brislington – and others in Horfield, Henbury and elsewhere. Dairying was a major occupation: milk and vegetables were sold to suppliers in the city and some farmers also supplied straw and hay for the city's large population of working horses. Farm labourers either lived in cottages on the farms or in the neighbouring village, and whilst the cottage exterior often suggested an idyllic existence those who took the trouble to look inside often found cramped and insanitary conditions every bit as bad as the city slums.

Shooting at Lawrence Weston Farm, Boxing Day, 1914. Clemant Hignell, tenant farmer of Lawrence Weston Farm from 1908 to 1917, is second from left in the bowler hat.

Westmorland Farm, Henbury, *c.* 1920. This 146 acre farm was let annually from the Sampsons of Henbury Manor. The farm supplied the stables of the Mansion House, residence of the Lord Mayor, with hay and straw; cider, cheese and bread were produced in the farmhouse until the 1930s.

Cottage at Coombe Dingle, *c.* 1875. An attractive winter scene with snow on the ground and a wisp of smoke rising from the chimney. Free from the dense housing of the old city and the new industrial suburbs, rural cottages could appear to offer an idyllic home environment: the reality was that many farm labourers' cottages were as overcrowded and insanitary as any urban slum.

The drawing room at Blaise Castle, *c.* 1900. Blaise Castle, designed by Robert Milne, was built as a summer house in about 1768 for Thomas Farr, owner of the Blaise Castle Estate from 1762 to 1778. For a short period after the First World War it provided unusual accommodation for C. Castell, a woodman on the estate, as no other cottages were available; he and his wife lived in the ground floor kitchen and used one of the towers as a bedroom.

Blaise Castle House, Henbury, 1870s. The house was built in 1796 by John Harford, a wealthy Bristol banker and merchant who had previously lived close to his business interests in Brunswick Square; this view from the south-east shows, from left, the original house designed by William Paty, the Ionic colonnade of Charles Cockerell's picture gallery built in 1832–33 and, right foreground, the elegant conservatory designed by John Nash in about 1806. The parkland, several hundred acres in extent, can be glimpsed in the background.

Mary Harford with her family at Blaise Castle House, 11 June 1909. This was Mary Harford's seventieth birthday and she is seen gathered with members of her family in front of a structure – now demolished – which linked the picture room with the conservatory; she is sixth from left, a tiny figure holding a posy of flowers, seated next to her son Frederick and his wife. Within a few years of Mary Harford's death in 1919, the Harfords had sold the estate to the City Council for recreational use.

Blaise Hamlet, Henbury, *c.* 1900. Designed by John Nash, the fashionable Regency architect, and George Repton in the Picturesque style, Blaise Hamlet was built between 1810 and 1811 by John Harford, owner of the Blaise Castle Estate, to provide homes for his estate workers and retired servants. The nine cottages were arranged informally around a village green; each one was different from its neighbour although all had towering chimneys of moulded brickwork. The result was one of the finest examples of picturesque cottage construction anywhere. The hamlet was soon established as a local Bristol beauty spot and was a popular subject with Victorian and Edwardian photographers.

Albert and Martha Jefferies outside their home, Circular Cottage, Blaise Hamlet, *c.* 1900. Albert Jefferies worked as a carter for the Harfords. Although the cottages were small they provided better accommodation than the average nineteenth-century farm labourer's cottage; each one had an oven, washing copper and privy.

A wealthy Bristol merchant in his country home: Richard Cripps with members of his family relaxing in the garden of The Grove, Wick Road, Brislington, *c.* 1880. Richard Cripps was an Italian marble importer with commercial premises on Redcliff Back.

The Grove, Wick Road, Brislington, *c.* 1880. This eighteenth-century house was the home of the Ricketts family, Bristol glass manufacturers from the late eighteenth century until 1862. From 1878 until 1899 it was occupied by Richard Cripps (left) and his family. The house survives as flats but the extensive gardens were built over with houses in Grove Park Road, Pendennis Park, Montrose Park and Bristol Hill.

RELIGION

A national religious census carried out in 1851 revealed that church attendance in Bristol was higher than in other cities of comparable size: roughly a third of the population regularly attended a church or chapel and this figure was being maintained thirty years later when the *Western Daily Press* carried out a local survey. Religion, therefore, was a major part of life in Victorian and Edwardian Bristol and through its response to the social problems created by the city's expansion exerted a strong influence on the city's development.

The 1851 census confirmed the supremacy of the Church of England which claimed 45.5 per cent of churchgoers and dominated the city's political life: 80 per cent of city councillors were Anglican. Nevertheless, the census also showed that the combined church attendance of the various Nonconformist denominations and the Roman Catholic Church accounted for 55.5 per cent of the total. Bristol had a long association with Protestant Dissent dating from the mid-seventeenth century, and was also closely associated with the origins of Methodism: John Wesley had established his first chapel in Bristol in 1739.

There were enormous differences – social as much as doctrinal – between the Established Church and some of the more extreme evangelical sects such as the Primitive Methodists. The parish church of St Andrew, Clifton, for example, was not a church for the poor man: 'he has no business there', wrote an observer in the 1840s, 'in that atmosphere of *eau de cologne* and *bouquet de la Reine.*' St Andrew's and a Wesleyan chapel in Bedminster or Easton attended by the labouring poor were worlds apart, but the second half of the nineteenth century saw some lowering of barriers between denominations. Dissenting Protestants had gained full political rights in 1828 and Roman Catholics in 1829 (Jews had to wait until 1858), and many wealthy and influential citizens, notably members of the Wills and Fry families were Nonconformist and played a leading part in municipal affairs.

All denominations were united in their mission to bring religion, temperance, cleanliness and improved standards of public behaviour to the urban masses. Horace Mann, the chief statistician of the 1851 census, stated that the 'labouring myriads, the masses of our working population . . . are but seldom seen in our religious congregations'. Voluntary organisations, closely supported by the city's clergy, which sought to 'civilise' the poor by distributing religious tracts and preaching, were active through the nineteenth century. There were also a number of temperance organisations such as the Bristol Temperance Society and the Band of Hope Union, which made the removal of drunkenness – seen by Victorian reformers as one of the great evils of the working class – their objective. Temperance hotels and coffee taverns were sponsored by the movements in an effort to attract the working class away from the beer houses. The Young Men's Christian Association, a Nonconformist organisation, was established in the city in 1853 with the objective of self improvement for young men, and once it began organising sports facilities its success was assured. Branches of the YMCA were opened in Bedminster, Easton, Fishponds, Hotwells and Totterdown.

Church leaders were concerned at the acute shortage, or absence altogether, of places of worship in the new suburbs. Church extension commissions helped to identify the areas where they were most needed, and between 1850 and 1919 the number of places of religious worship of all denominations increased from 83 to about 260. The number of Church of England places of worship more than doubled over this period. Clifton acquired several new Anglican churches after 1850: St Paul's in 1853 and then two in the 1860s – All Saints', Pembroke Road and Emmanuel, Guthrie Road – built as a response to the development of Clifton then taking place towards the Downs; St Anselm's, Whately Road, followed in 1897. New churches were also added in the affluent areas of Stoke Bishop and Leigh Woods. In Bedminster the parish church of St John's, a small seventeenth-century structure, was replaced by a new larger church in 1855, and by 1910 another nine Anglican churches had been built in Bedminster, Totterdown and Knowle. Several new churches had been opened in the new eastern industrial suburbs in the 1840s – in Barton Hill, Easton and Montpelier – and between 1850 and 1909 another fourteen were added. St Werburgh's, one of the old city churches, was relocated from Corn Street to Mina Road in 1879. St Philip's Marsh acquired a parish church, St Silas's, in 1867, and a church was opened in Avonmouth in 1893. St Agnes's, Newfoundland Road, consecrated in 1886, cost £5,000, half of which was donated by Clifton College which had established a mission there in 1875. Several other churches in the centre and Clifton followed this example and adopted poor areas, carrying out missionary work and providing financial support for new churches: thus, St Paul's, Clifton, helped finance the building of St Michael and All Angels, Windmill Hill, in 1886.

The expansion of the Nonconformist denominations followed similar lines. The number of Baptist chapels in this period increased from seven to twenty-six and the affluent congregation of the Buckingham Baptist chapel in Clifton took on missionary work in Hotwells. Congregational church building had been vigorous in the mid-nineteenth century when Arley chapel, Cheltenham Road and Highbury chapel, Cotham were built, but lost momentum until the end of the century when an extension movement stimulated the building of new places of worship in Brislington, Bedminster, Henleaze and Avonmouth. Both the Baptists and the Congregationalists built new training colleges in Cotham in the early 1900s. The industrial suburbs, where the evangelical message of Methodism exerted a strong hold amongst the poor, also acquired many new chapels; by 1919 there were over sixty belonging to the various Methodist churches. The expansion of Roman Catholicism was slower, however, and in 1919 there were only ten churches besides a few convents in the city.

The building of new churches and the restoration of older churches was the visible manifestation of the energy of the various religious bodies in Victorian and Edwardian Bristol. Whilst providing for the religious needs of the growing population they were also built to enhance the physical environment. The public appeal for the restoration of St Mary Redcliffe, published in 1842, was intended to create 'a national monument of unequalled beauty'. New imposing churches were an important feature of the Victorian reworking of the city: new towers and spires appeared on the skyline, whilst in the poorer suburbs the small stone chapels with a traceried window facing the street provided welcome relief from the drab rows of terraces and factories. From the mid-nineteenth century Gothic came to be regarded as the only true Christian architecture, and after the mid-century swept alternative styles – Grecian and Italianate – to one side. The designs were mostly conceived as accurate representations of medieval ecclesiastical architecture: Buckingham Baptist chapel, designed by the local architect Richard Shackleton Pope, with its soaring pinnacles, sharply pointed blank arcading and rose window was a successful essay in the Continental High Gothic manner, and was generally admired upon its completion in 1847. Beautifully proportioned and carefully detailed designs in Early English and Decorated Gothic by John Norton, a London architect, were provided for the replacement church of St John's, Bedminster, St Mary Magdelene, Stoke Bishop, and Holy Trinity, Stapleton.

Norton also designed the spire added to Christ Church, Clifton, in 1859. Church spires were an important and conspicuous element of Victorian Gothic architecture. The replacement of the spire of St Mary Redcliffe, that 'splendid, heavenly pointing member', in the words of the 1842 appeal, was seen as the crowning glory of the restored church; it would bear comparison, it was confidently asserted, with some of the finest in Europe including Strasbourg, Salisbury and Norwich. Religion, aesthetics and civic pride became intertwined. The restoration and expansion of the Cathedral was a matter of practical expediency – the church was simply too small – but it was also of general concern that the city lacked a cathedral of sufficient grandeur, and so the appeal to enlarge the Cathedral and provide it with two west towers received support from leading Nonconformists as well as Anglicans in the city. Anglican churches, in particular, lacking a tower and especially a spire were seen to be incomplete: John Latimer, writing in 1887 of All Saints', Pembroke Road, Clifton, an ornate and massive structure by the London architect George Edmund Street, remarked that (lacking its tower and spire through want of funds), 'the church viewed from a distance, presents the appearance of a gigantic barn'. All Saints' eventually acquired a tower but two churches by John Norton, Emmanuel, Clifton, and St John's, Bedminster, never acquired a spire.

Church building was not simply a matter of show and prestige. Religion and particularly doctrinal issues were also important in deciding architectural details, and there were several major disputes which exposed some of the deep differences between the High and Low Church factions within the Church of England. In 1855 the erection of a richly sculptured reredos in the new church of St John's, Bedminster, created a storm of protest from Low Church clergy who saw it as 'papistical'. Some twenty years later a similar reaction was provoked during the restoration of the cathedral, when statues above the north porch were given cardinals' hats by the sculptor: Low Church supporters claimed they were an insult to Protestantism and the Dean, Gilbert Elliot, a prominent low churchman, had them torn down. Divisive tendencies persisted throughout the period. When a United Thanksgiving service to mark the end of the First World War was held in the Cathedral on 20 November 1918, some clergy protested against the participation of the Pastor of Highbury Congregational Church; making no apology, the Bishop replied that this was a united service for all Christians.

Nevertheless, the city now had an enlarged cathedral and the bishopric and diocese which had been split in 1836 was restored in 1897. Throughout the city, there were many new churches and chapels to cater for the spiritual needs of a city where religion remained an important force in shaping the future.

Abbey gateway, May 1858. The Augustinian Abbey, founded in 1140 by Robert Fitzharding, a prominent Bristol citizen was established as the cathedral in 1542 when the diocese of Bristol was formed. When the abbey was suppressed by Henry VIII in 1539 work was underway on rebuilding the nave but this was stopped and until the mid-nineteenth century the cathedral could only accommodate a congregation of 300. In 1836 the diocese was combined with Gloucester and it was commonly said that Bristol had only half a cathedral and half a diocese!

This early photograph shows the late Norman Abbey gateway with the Dean's house on the left and the Precentor's house on the right. Part of the Deanery was demolished in the 1860s when Deanery Road was created and the rest went shortly after 1901 to make way for the new Central Library; the Precentor's house was carefully removed when the gateway was restored in 1885. (J.W.G. Gutch)

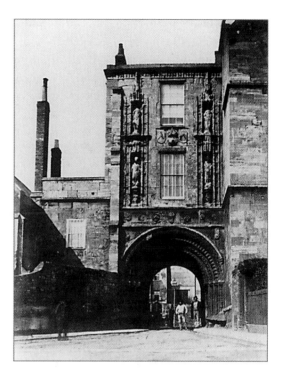

Bristol Cathedral, c. 1910. The cathedral was restored and considerably enlarged from the late 1860s. Much restoration of the old fabric was carried out, but it was the addition of a nave and two western towers designed by G.E. Street which transformed the exterior, giving Bristol, at last, a cathedral befitting the city. Work began in 1868 and the nave was completed in 1877, and the towers in 1888, although without the steeples of Street's design.

St Mary Magdelene (Church of England), Stoke Bishop, *c*. 1875. This church, designed by John Norton, was built in 1860 to provide a parish church for the growing population of Stoke Bishop. The tower and spire were added in 1872. Members of the Wills family and Sir George White, director of the tramway company and founder of the Bristol Aircraft Company, are buried in the churchyard.

Interior of Emmanuel church (Church of England), Guthrie Road, Clifton, *c*. 1910. Another design by John Norton, this Anglican church close to Clifton College was consecrated in 1869. A large tower was subsequently added but plans for a spire were never realised; the church no longer exists although the tower is incorporated in a modern block of flats called Emmanuel Court.

St Mary Redcliffe, *c.* 1875. The church lost its first spire in a storm in 1445 and the capstone of the replacement was laid by the mayor W. Proctor Baker in May 1872.

St John's (Church of England), Bedminster, before 1857. This old parish church, which the Bristol historian John Latimer described in 1887 as a 'mean edifice of the seventeenth century, capable of holding only 450 persons' was replaced by a new larger church, an example of High Victorian Gothic by John Norton. The last service in the old church was held on 25 June 1854 and it was demolished in 1857 after the replacement had been consecrated.

St Andrew's church, Clifton, c. 1910. This was the parish church of Clifton. It was designed by James Foster and built in 1819–22 replacing a seventeenth-century church, itself the replacement of an earlier church. The church was badly damaged in the Blitz on the night of 24 November 1940, and although the 112 ft high tower survived it was pulled down in 1954.

Interior of St Mary's-on-the-Quay (Roman Catholic), Colston Avenue, *c.* 1910. This church with its impressive Corinthian portico has been a familiar landmark on the Quay, and subsequently Colston Avenue, since 1839. It was designed by Richard Shackleton Pope as a chapel for the Irvingites – an evangelical sect – but shortly after its construction was purchased by the Roman Catholic Church. The interior, seen here, is no less impressive with giant columns dominating the chancel.

Greenbank Cemetery, *c.* 1912. This cemetery, belonging to St Philip's parish, was consecrated on 14 April 1871 and extended in 1880. The chapel with its polygonal turret was designed by Henry Masters and built in 1870. It came under municipal control in 1896 when the City Council became the burial board for the entire city.

Buckingham Baptist chapel, Queen's Road, *c.* 1910. Designed by Richard Shackleton Pope, this church, built in the continental High Gothic manner and opened on 2 June 1847, was described by one critic as 'a particularly chaste and beautiful Gothic building'.

Arley chapel (Congregational), Cheltenham Road, *c.* 1905. Here the architects, Foster & Wood, resorted to the Italianate for this Congregational church built in 1855 to serve new suburbs north of the centre. It now serves as a Polish church.

Western College, Cotham Road, *c.* 1910. Western College was founded to train Congregational ministers; this attractive example of Edwardian Jacobean architecture designed by H. Dare Bryan was opened on 27 September 1906. A similar training institution for the Baptists was established at Stokes Croft and moved to Woodland Road in 1915. The building now serves as a family practice.

Salvation Army Citadel, Ashley Road, built in 1896. The fortress-like Salvation Army headquarters was built in 1896, the centre of operations for General Booth's army – saving souls amongst the 'submerged tenth' of the population; those who somehow existed on incomes below the subsistence level. In 1881 the Salvation Army claimed 15.4 per cent of the church-going population in Bristol.

James Cox (1838–1900), home missionary, c. 1890. Born at Westbury, Wiltshire, James Cox worked as a furnace man at the Ashton Ironworks until a foundry explosion left him crippled and blind. He spent nearly a year recovering from his injuries at the Bristol General Hospital, an experience that changed his life: previously a heavy drinker and keeper of bad company he turned to Christianity. Upon his recovery he was led on crutches to a Wesleyan chapel in Bedminster; he learned to read type for the blind and started work as a missionary, visiting the sick and blind and holding prayer meetings in his small terraced house – 30 Sion Road, Bedminster. He also held open-air meetings at which he played hymns on a portable harmonium (now preserved at Blaise Castle House Museum, Bristol), and with others founded a mission band which as the Cycle Mission Band was continued by one of his sons. It is seen here in the early 1900s.

CORPORATE BRISTOL

T he second half of the nineteenth century saw a greater involvement of local government in the running of the city. The Municipal Corporations Act of 1835 had transferred existing responsibilities for law and order from the old parish authorities to the City Council. From the mid-nineteenth century new national legislation invested the Council with new responsibilities: for health (for example, building sewers and public baths), enforcing building regulations, and maintaining parks, libraries, the Museum and the Art Gallery. The Council also assumed control of cemeteries in 1896 and after the Education Act of 1902 took over the running of schools. Each function was managed by its own committee, and after 1850 these multiplied so that by the early twentieth century there were thirty running the city's affairs.

Through the second half of the nineteenth century Bristol's leading industrialists such as Christopher Thomas, soap maker, and Thomas Proctor, bone merchant and dealer in manure, dominated local government, chairing committees and serving as aldermen and mayor. Until 1882 only those owning property worth more than £1,000 or occupying property of a rateable value of £30 or more were eligible for election. Before the Municipal Franchise Act of 1869 only about 3 to 10 per cent of the population were qualified to vote; thus a middle-class electorate produced a middle-class council. Boundary changes in the late nineteenth and early twentieth century increased the area governed by the city by over four times. The number of wards increased from ten in the 1850s to twenty three by 1907, whilst the number of elected councillors rose from forty-eight to sixty-nine although the distribution of councillors was uneven, favouring the prosperous and influential wards like Clifton. Nevertheless, as the vote was progressively extended, the Council became less socially exclusive and came to represent a wider cross-section of Bristol's population.

The City Council's officials were surrounded by a considerable degree of civic tradition and ceremony which had its roots in Bristol's medieval local government, although following the reforms of 1835 the number of ceremonial officials was reduced to make financial savings. The post of City Crier was abolished in 1890 and the office of Exchange Keeper in 1893. The Council did not invest in new council offices like so many other Victorian towns and cities, and had to squeeze its expanding business into the small and inconvenient Council House of 1825, which occupied a less than imposing site in Corn Street. However, the city acquired a new impressive Mansion House, the home of the mayor, in Clifton Down in 1874 thanks to the gift of Alderman Thomas Proctor, and in 1899 civic prestige was further strengthened when Queen Victoria conferred the title of Lord Mayor upon Sir Herbert Ashman, an honour already bestowed on the mayor of Birmingham and several other northern towns.

The Municipal Corporations Act of 1835 ordered boroughs throughout England and Wales to appoint a paid professional police force. The new force was established in 1836 with 227 officers led by a superintendent based at four police stations at Wine Street, Bedminster, Brandon Hill and Trinity Road, St Philips. A new central police station was built at the Bridewell in 1844, and the same year the river police was formed to protect merchant shipping and protect cargoes from fire and theft. In the late 1870s the police took over responsibility for fire protection throughout the city from the insurance companies, and a new city fire brigade was established with its own superintendent and twelve policemen. In 1880 the first full time detective staff – one inspector and seven detectives – were appointed. As the city grew, new police stations were added in the suburbs and allotted to the original four divisions. 'A' Division included the Bridewell station, the Water Police and Horfield station; 'B' Division comprised Bedminster, Brislington and Knowle; 'C' Division came to include Brandon Hill, Westbury-on-Trym, Redland, Stoke Bishop, Shirehampton and Avonmouth; whilst 'D' Division combined Trinity Road and stations at St George, Eastville and Fishponds. In 1898 the fire brigade was also expanded to cover the newly incorporated districts.

Hospital provision was already established in Bristol by the mid-nineteenth century but continued to expand to meet the demands of the growing population. The Society of Friends had established the General Hospital in a house in Guinea Street in 1832 with accommodation for thirty beds, but it was soon proving inadequate to treat the growing number of industrial accidents from the docks and from factories and collieries in Bedminster and Ashton. A new larger hospital was built from 1853 and when the main block opened in 1858 it had space for 150 beds, which was increased to 200 when a new wing was opened in 1891. The Bristol Royal Infirmary, founded in 1735, also increased its capacity in the later nineteenth century. By the early twentieth century the hospital was heavily in debt; it was rescued from its difficulties by Sir George White, managing director of the Bristol Tramways & Carriage Company, following his election as President and Treasurer in 1904. White organised an energetic programme of fund raising to clear the debt and also to finance the building of a new extension, a plain and uncompromisingly modern block designed by Charles Holden which was named the Edward VII Memorial Infirmary and opened on 28 June 1912. Support from leading industrial and commercial figures like White was an important factor in the expansion of hospital provision in Victorian and Edwardian Bristol. The Children's Hospital on St Michael's Hill largely owed its existence to the efforts of Mark Whitwill; and Joseph Storrs Fry, who served as President of the General Hospital, provided financial support together with E.P. Wills towards establishing the Queen Victoria Convalescent Home on Durdham Down, opened by the Queen in 1899.

In the mid-nineteenth century the care of the destitute, the old and infirm, the mentally ill and others unable to look after themselves rested with three Poor Law Unions – for Bristol, Bedminster and Clifton – and each had its own workhouse to provide indoor relief. The Bristol authority, the Board of Guardians, was established in 1696 and had adapted an ornate timber-framed merchant's house, St Peter's Hospital, as the city's workhouse and lunatic asylum. In the 1830s, to relieve severe overcrowding in St Peter's Hospital, a former prison for French prisoners of war at Stapleton was obtained for use as a workhouse. The Bedminster and Clifton Unions, which were also responsible for poor relief in some of the neighbouring rural parishes, established workhouses at Flax Bourton and Eastville. In 1898 a new Union for the whole of Bristol came into being, and that year there were 2,357 inmates in the workhouses formerly administered by the old authorities.

That same year, 1898, the twenty-two almshouses scattered across the city provided homes for 377 people. No other British city was so well provided with such charitable institutions: some had medieval origins – like Foster's almshouses, dating to 1483, whilst Lady Haberfield's almshouses in Hotwells were founded in 1891. The founders often aimed to benefit a particular type of person – thus Sarah Ridley's almshouses founded in 1739 were expressly for bachelors and spinsters. The Blue Maids' Orphanage had been founded in 1795 to care for some forty orphan girls: photographs of the orphanage in the 1890s are featured in this section, but at the time it was overshadowed by the considerably larger orphanage on Ashley Down founded by the Rev. George Muller in 1849, which housed 2,000 children by the 1880s.

In 1870, the year of the Education Act, a survey into educational provision in Bristol recorded 236 elementary schools in Bristol; the survey also highlighted the shortage of school places in the poorer parishes and estimated that about a third of children aged between five and ten years were not attending any school. By the terms of the 1870 Act a publicly elected school board with rate-aid was established in 1871, and immediately turned its attention to providing schools in the new industrial suburbs: in 1874 a school was built in St Philips, and the following year a school for 750 children was opened at Barton Hill. The new schools were undenominational – this was bitterly opposed by the Church of England and Conservatives – but some rudimentary teaching of the Bible was included in the curriculum and physical drill to promote proper conduct was instilled in a disciplined manner. Other Board schools were built in Bedminster, Ashton Gate, Hotwells, Redland and Baptist Mills, whilst some existing schools were taken over. By 1902, when the City Council took over responsibility for education from the School Board, average attendance was not far below 90 per cent.

There were several endowed schools providing secondary education, including the Queen Elizabeth's Hospital School and the Grammar School (see page 127). Both dated from the sixteenth century and acquired impressive buildings on new sites in the nineteenth century: Queen Elizabeth's Hospital was provided with a Tudor collegiate-style school on Brandon Hill, designed by Thomas Foster & Son and completed in 1847, whilst the Grammar School's new building at Tyndall's Park was opened in 1880. Clifton College was founded as a public school by the Clifton College Company. Charles Frederick Hansom designed the school, which opened in 1862 with fifty-eight boys; a handsome Gothic chapel was added four years later. Gothic architecture was considered appropriate for the education of young Christian gentlemen. The school's first headmaster, the Rev. John Percival, believed the school should serve the city at large and was closely involved in establishing the University, evening classes and missionary work amongst the poor.

The Lord Mayor's Chapel, College Green, *c*. 1912. Otherwise known as St Mark's, it was originally the chapel of the thirteenth-century Gaunt's Hospital. The chapel was purchased by the Corporation in 1541 and established as their official place of worship in 1722; it is the only civic church in the country. A thorough restoration in 1888–9 created its present-day external appearance.

The annual Rush Sunday Service at St Mary Redcliffe with the Lord Mayor, Edward Robinson, Whit-Sunday, 1909. The service is held in commemoration of William Canynge, a leading Bristol merchant of the fifteenth century who later entered the Church. A special service is preached in the presence of the Lord Mayor and rushes are strewn on the ground.

Ridleys Almshouse, Milk Street, *c.* 1900. Founded in 1739 by Sarah Ridley, this was one of over twenty almshouses in Bristol in the second half of the nineteenth century; in Mathew's 1864 Bristol Directory, it is described as having places for 'five bachelors and five maids', each receiving 9*s* fortnightly. The city watch box on the corner, used by nightwatchmen, was built in 1820 and demolished in August 1913 after a period of use as a shop.

Joseph Croot, City Crier from 1855 until 1890, when the post was abolished. He wore a livery of black coat with brass buttons bearing the Bristol coat of arms, tricorn hat, blue velvet breeches and gaiters.

Police Constabulary 'A' Division tug of war team, champions of the West of England and South Wales, 1907. 'A' Division was based at the Central Station, Bridewell. Back row from left, Ashford, PC Hook (Vice Capt.), PC Robbins, PC Froud; middle row: PS Hill (Trainer), PC Harding (Vice Capt.), PC Dyer, PC Gully, PC Grant, PS Clapp; seated: Inspector G. London, Mr C. Croker, Deputy Chief Constable, Mr J. Cann, Chief Constable, Inspector R. Pope, Inspector G. Harris (Capt.) The Chief Constable is wearing his day uniform. (R. Pratchett, 130 Cheltenham Road, Bristol)

Bristol Constabulary Fire Brigade, Central Station, 1882. Officers stand alongside their Merryweather horse-drawn steam fire engine: Engineer Prouting, left, Superintendent Wingfield, centre front, First Coachman Pearce holding the reins and Second Coachman Shipp on the right, and five officers: Wergen, Smith, James, Durrant and Martin (from left to right on the engine). Merryweather, an old-established London firm, were leading makers of fire engines. The type shown here used steam from the engine to drive the pump.

Bristol General Hospital, Guinea Street, *c*. 1915. This imposing building of grey Pennant stone and Bath stone was built from 1853 on the site of the former Guinea Street hospital established in 1830. Designed by W.B. Gingell, it was an early example of the 'Bristol Byzantine' style adopted for many large buildings in the city during the 1860s and 1870s. The basement formed dockside warehouses, which provided an extra source of income. This view dates from after 1912 when a southern wing, seen here on the right, was built over the terraced extension of the warehouse basement.

Prince – canine friend of the Bristol General Hospital. This dog, owned by Alfred William Collins, persuaded many customers entering his master's shellfish bar in Colston Avenue to make a donation in his collections box for the Royal General Hospital, and between 1915 and his death in 1924 raised over £37.

The Royal Hospital for Sick Children and Women, St Michael's Hill, 1890s. The hospital was established in 1866 to treat children under twelve years of age, women 'suffering from diseases peculiar to their sex' and to improve knowledge of child-care especially among the poor. Originally housed in the Royal Fort, the Gothic style premises shown here, designed by Robert Carwen, were built in 1885. In this photograph, convalescing children are seen on the lawn outside the hospital holding toys and dolls, with several nurses in attendance.

King Edward Memorial Building, Royal Infirmary, Upper Maudlin Street, c. 1915. This was one of the earliest of provincial hospitals, founded in 1735. Sir George White, the dynamic and forward thinking director of the tramway company, rescued the hospital from debt after he became President and Treasurer in 1904. With his backing this new large block, designed by H. Percy Adams and Charles Holden, was opened in 1912.

St Peter's Hospital, late nineteenth century. This remarkably ornate timber-framed house beside St Peter's church was first mentioned in 1402 and rebuilt in 1612 by Robert Aldworth, a prominent merchant and several times mayor. After serving as a mint during the re-coinage of 1696–8 it was then purchased by the Bristol Corporation of the Poor (i.e. the Board of Guardians responsible for poor relief) for use as a workhouse for the destitute and as a lunatic asylum. From the 1830s it was replaced by a larger workhouse at Stapleton and after 1865 used mainly for administrative purposes. It was destroyed during the Blitz of 24 November 1940 – arguably Bristol's greatest architectural loss of the Second World War.

Blue Coat School, Henbury, 1870s. A charity school founded in the early seventeenth century, which was rebuilt in 1830. In 1869 the school was providing elementary education for sixty boys including seven boarders. The 1871 national census records the master as Henry Pillenger, while there were seven 'boy scholars' aged between ten and fourteen boarding at the adjacent Henbury School House.

South Street Schools, Bedminster, c. 1912. Designed by the Bristol architect W.V. Gouch, this school was built by the Bristol School Board in 1894. It originally had nineteen classrooms and three separate yards for boys, girls and infants.

Blue Maids' Asylum for Poor Orphan Girls, Ashley Hill, 1890s. This orphanage was established in 1795 to 'rescue destitute girls from idleness and vice, qualifying them for servants in respectable families'. The building shown here was built in about 1828 and suggests that orphan girls here grew up in a much pleasanter environment than those living in George Muller's barracks-like orphanage on Ashley Down.

Morning lessons at Blue Maids' Orphanage, 1890s. The schoolmistress (see also opposite) is sitting on the left, some of the girls are sewing but others, holding slates, may be grappling with the arithmetic of the problem chalked on the blackboard. The 1891 national census records forty-two girls in the orphanage ranging in age from five to sixteen years. Embroidery made by the girls was sold to supplement the income from donations and legacies.

The kitchen, Blue Maids' Orphanage, 1890s. It is 11.25 a.m., the cook is peeling apples and has the help of three girls who are probably glad to be spared the sewing and the arithmetic lesson. Compare the simple flat flame gas burner fitted here with the more ornate lamp in the study, which appears to be a combined paraffin and gas lamp.

The study or drawing room at Blue Maids' Orphanage, 1890s. The woman on the left is almost certainly Isolene Lee, a native of Weymouth born in about 1848, matron of the orphanage from 1887 to 1919; the woman netting on the right may be Anne Miller, who was the schoolmistress at the orphanage in 1891. The orphanage closed in about 1926.

Net practice at Clifton College, late 1860s. Sport became an important part of life in the school, and cricket the pre-eminent sport up to the First World War. The imposing Gothic buildings were designed by Charles Frederick Hansom, the Big School prominent in this view was opened in 1862 and the chapel completed in 1866; a tower and north aisle were added later to the chapel.

Queen Elizabeth Hospital School from the corner of Jacob's Wells Road and John Carr's Terrace, c. 1910. The City School or Queen Elizabeth's Hospital was founded by John Carr, an Elizabethan soap maker, in 1586. Built in 1847 of red Brandon grit from the site on which it was built, the school rises fortress-like on the western side of Brandon Hill. The red brick house, below, built in about 1894, provided accommodation for the school's stable keeper.

ARTS & LEISURE

The modernisation of the city widened opportunities for leisure: new forms of entertainment and recreation were added to the old. Music halls, cinemas, parks and open spaces were created and new cultural facilities such as libraries, a museum and an art gallery established. There were several major factors governing the rise of new types of leisure: technological innovations, higher levels of popular education and, as in other areas of the city's development, leisure also benefited from greater municipal involvement.

There were inevitably social differences in forms of leisure and entertainment. The appeal of the theatre was strongest amongst the middle classes: thus the New Theatre Royal opened in Park Row by James Henry Shute, owner of the Theatre Royal, who recognised the demand from theatre-goers in the fashionable suburbs for a theatre closer to home than the old Theatre Royal in King Street. Better known as the Princes Theatre, it became Bristol's most fashionable theatre. In the mid-nineteenth century the recreation and entertainment of poorer citizens centred on drink, informal activities and occasional visits from fairs and circuses. The new forms of leisure, however, saw greater formality as halls were established for the performance of more organised entertainments. The largest and most important was Colston Hall, opened in 1867, which became the focal point of musical life in the city. The increasing mass appeal of music was also reflected by the rise of the music hall. The earliest were tavern music halls: they served drink and were the subject of disapproval from Nonconformists and the Temperance movement, but in the 1890s the reputation of music halls was transformed by the opening of the People's Palace, Baldwin Street, and the Empire Theatre in Old Market. Unlike the tavern music halls they were teetotal – although entrance to the Empire Theatre, Old Market, was through the doors of a public house – the White Hart! The old music halls could not compete: the last to go was the Tivoli in

Broadmead, which ran into financial difficulties and closed in 1900. The new music halls were respectable; they were family places of entertainment and with seating capacities of about 3,000 they had to have a broad appeal. With them the age of popular mass entertainment had arrived.

The music halls were also the first establishments to introduce a new novelty – the cinematograph. The last of the old tavern music halls, the Tivoli, was the first to show the moving picture in 1896. They were soon being shown at other venues including the Colston Hall and the People's Palace, and from 1908 purpose-built cinemas appeared, the first being the Bio in Counterslip; thereafter the popularity of the cinema increased rapidly and by 1919 there were some thirty-four across the city.

Greater organisation also permeated sport. Team games like cricket, rugby football and association football increased in popularity within a framework of regional and nationally recognised leagues. New clubs were created and with them new heroes, such as W.G. Grace. Born in Downend in 1848, Grace captained the Gloucestershire County Cricket Club from its formation in 1870 until 1899 and in his prime was the most idolised sportsman in Britain. The growth of organised sports was helped by shorter working hours, improvements in transport and also by cheap press and sporting publications which generated popular interest. cycling was another pastime which benefitted from improvements in the design of the bicycle. Archery and tennis also became popular from the 1870s – with women as well as men, although sports that required equipment tended to remain the preserve of the middle classes. Association football, however, enjoyed widespread appeal, and from the 1880s developed as the spectator sport of the urban masses.

The involvement of municipal government in providing parks and public baths was born of the concern for the health of citizens living in areas of dense housing. Parks were established by the City Council, particularly from the 1880s, until by the early 1900s there were thirty-eight parks, open spaces and commons maintained by the city. New parks such as the 70 acres of Eastville Park, acquired in 1887, and Victoria Park in Bedminster (see page 61), 57 acres in extent, provided important green spaces within a smoke-filled, crowded industrial environment. Besides providing fresh air, parks were used for physical exercise whilst music could be enjoyed from a bandstand – a common feature of the Victorian park. Swimming baths were originally seen as a way of keeping the working classes clean, and then interest in swimming as a sport emerged in the 1870s; the Council built prestigious new baths at Jacobs Wells in 1884. Municipal administration was next extended to the arts when the Council assumed control of the Museum in 1894, and in 1905 the Art Gallery, the gift of Lord Winterstoke to the city, was opened.

Royal West of England Academy, Queen's Road, 1870s. This Italianate building designed by John Hirst was built in 1854 for the joint use of the Bristol Academy of Fine Arts and the Bristol Society of Architects.

Ernest Board (1877–1934) painting the marriage of William Penn and Hannah Callowhill at the Friends' Meeting House, the Friary, Bristol, completed in 1916. Board lived at The Elms, Ashley Hill. He was a prolific artist in oils and watercolours, and his paintings of great moments in the history of Bristol reflected Bristol's civic pride in the early twentieth century.

View from the stage in the Princes Theatre, Park Row, *c.* 1910. Opened as the New Theatre Royal in 1867 by James Henry Shute, owner of the Theatre Royal, as a response to the demand from theatre-goers in the fashionable suburbs for a theatre closer to home than the old Theatre Royal in King Street. It became Bristol's most fashionable theatre, but was destroyed by enemy action in 1940.

Colston Hall, *c.* 1910. The Colston Hall Co. was launched in the mid-1860s to provide Bristol with a large concert hall capable of taking the large orchestras then on tour. The building designed by Foster & Wood was finally opened on 20 September 1867 and W.H. Wills provided the organ, which cost £3,000. The hall gave a great boost to the musical life of the city, and in 1873 Bristol held its first music festival.

The Coliseum Picture House, Park Row, one of Bristol's early cinemas. It opened in August 1912 but did not survive the arrival of the 'talkies' in the 1920s. It was also used as a skating rink and dance hall, and during the First World War seaplanes for the Admiralty and Avro biplanes were assembled here by Parnall & Sons.

Bedminster Hippodrome, East Street, c. 1911. This imposing music hall seating 3,000 was opened by Walter de Freece in July 1911, but soon ran into difficulties and was taken over by Oswald Stoll, builder of the new Bristol Hippodrome, St Augustine's Parade; he converted it to a cinema in May 1915 and in March 1918 it was renamed the Stoll Picture House – one of five cinemas in the Bedminster area by 1919. The constable is from 'B' Division based in Bedminster.

Street organ in St Philip's Marsh, *c.* 1905. Music was an important feature of popular street entertainment until finally drowned out by the noise of motor vehicle traffic during the 1920s.

Entrance lodge to the Zoological gardens, Clifton, *c.* 1915. The gardens, occupying 12 acres, were established by the Bristol & Clifton Zoological Society in 1835. The original subscribers included I.K. Brunel, W.D. & H.O. Wills, members of the Fry family and John Harford of Blaise Castle House, Henbury (see page 88).

Gentlemen cricketers of the Rockleaze cricket team, *c.* 1875. Cricket flourished in Victorian Bristol, particularly in the affluent suburbs.

St Philip's Football Club, 1906. The popularity of association football was strongest in the industrial suburbs. Henry Webb, son of the landlord of the Victoria, St Philip's Marsh, and later landlord himself of the Rising Sun, Lower Castle Street, is on the middle row, second left.

John Webb, landlord of the Victoria, with his wife Mary in a donkey and trap outside the back door of the public house in Victoria Terrace, St Philip's Marsh, *c.* 1909.

An Edwardian picnic: Dorothy (left) and Frances Brewer (second from right) with their mother of 6 West Park, Cotham, and two friends, Connie Stroud and Kathleen Bishop, *c.* 1910.

BRISTOL & THE GREAT WAR

War with Germany was declared on 4 August 1914. It was holiday time. Excursion trains were cancelled to enable the movement of troops; soldiers of the Gloucestershire Regiment based at Horfield Barracks, the Territorial Forces and members of the Royal Naval Reserve were mobilised immediately. The one German ship in the port was seized and her crew detained. Amongst the civilian population, the fear that food would soon run out caused panic: there were queues at the shops and prices rose. The fears, however, were unfounded as the Government moved quickly to control prices.

Over the next four years, until the signing of the Armistice on 11 November 1918, Bristol played a major part in what quickly became the 'Great War'. Unprecedented in its world-wide repercussions and in many ways novel, it was the first to be fought by the entire nation and not merely the armed forces. For the first time, the highly organised states of the last century were able to command the energies of all citizens to mobilise the productive capacity of modern industries towards the war effort and also to call upon the resources of modern technology to find new methods of destruction and defence. Many Bristolians were directly involved in the military effort: some 60,000 men from Bristol served in the wars and at least 4,000 were killed. Rolls of honour became a regular feature of church services whilst the *Western Daily Press* carried hundreds of obituaries of men killed in the fighting. Many women were enrolled into national service and served in the hospitals caring for the wounded; within the first month of the war, trained nurses from the Royal Infirmary were dispatched for service at the front.

The first hospital train bringing wounded soldiers to the city arrived at Temple Meads on 2 September 1914, returning 120 men from Mons. They were treated at the Second Southern Hospital set up by the War Office, which consisted of the new wing of the Royal Infirmary opened in 1912 together with a new infirmary at Southmead; it was soon augmented by Bishop's Knoll in Stoke Bishop, the home of Robert and Margery Bush which they converted to a hospital of a hundred beds. In 1916 the Red Maids' School at Westbury-on-Trym was converted to a hospital and auxiliary hospitals under the Red Cross were set up in the Bristol area. Many voluntary organisations, besides, assisted in the care of the sick and wounded.

The war saw a huge increase in incoming tonnage through the port from foreign countries: the wounded returned on hospital ships through the port whilst troops and equipment were dispatched by sea – the port played a significant role, for example, in supplying the Gallipoli expedition in 1915. Many local industries contributed to the war effort. Shipbuilding in Bristol was not in a thriving state in 1914 but by 1916 the need to replace shipping lost to German submarine attacks generated new work. Charles Hill & Sons, the city's leading shipbuilders, constructed additional berths at their Albion yard to cope with the extra demand. The city's newly established aero industry also played a major role. The British and Colonial Aeroplane Company, established only four years before war broke out, manufactured hundreds of aircraft for use during the war including 376 Bristol Scouts and the versatile Bristol Fighter, which played an important part in the later stages of the war. From 1915 the Bristol firm Parnall & Sons commenced aircraft manufacture, using the Coliseum in Park Row for assembly. Douglas Motors Ltd supplied motocycles for war use. John Lysaght Ltd, manufacturers of galvanised iron, made thousands of Nissen huts, wire netting and other galvanised ware. Christopher Thomas & Bros and other soap makers produced dynamite glycerine and the Bristol Gas Company supplied benzol and toluol for use in high explosives. Wills and Fry's turned to the manufacture of shells whilst their tobacco and chocolate was sent to the troops on the front. The clothing manufacturers and boot makers in the district supplied military clothing; it was reckoned that some three to four million Bristol-made boots were supplied to troops worldwide. Women took the place of men who had gone to war: they were introduced on the trams in December 1916 and by March 1917 the Bristol Tramways & Carriage Company had 800 women filling men's places.

When news of an armistice reached the city, there was spontaneous public rejoicing. Many people imagined that life would settle down to something like it had been before, but with the Great War a whole epoch had come to an end.

Soldiers marching in Park Row as passengers on board a tram from Westbury-on-Trym look on, 7 September 1914. According to the reverse inscription of this postcard, these were students from the University 'marching to camp at Barrow'. The Coliseum in the background was soon to be used for the assembly of fighter aircraft.

The 4th Gloucesters, some still in civilian clothes, training in the grounds of Bristol Grammar School, 1914. The school voluntarily gave up its playing field in Tyndall's Park, which was used extensively for training purposes.

Margery and Robert Bush who converted their home, Bishop's Knoll in Stoke Bishop, to a wartime hospital at their own expense. It received its first patients from 13 September 1914 and was the only privately owned hospital in the country to receive wounded soldiers directly from the Front.

The Motor Cycle Club taking convalescing soldiers for a ride, *c.* 1919. The King Edward Memorial Building became part of the War Office's Second Southern Hospital on the outbreak of the First World War and treated 20,000 sick and wounded soldiers as in-patients and 50,000 as out-patients. Organised outings to the country, the zoo, the Museum and Art Gallery and local music halls were arranged to give recovering soldiers a change of scenery.

Captured German submarines U86 and UC92 on view to the public in St Augustine's Reach in December 1918. German submarines caused extensive loss of allied shipping during the war, including merchant vessels and hospital ships on their way to Bristol.

Bristol Peace Celebrations Certificate presented to all schoolchildren in Bristol on 24 July 1919.

ACKNOWLEDGEMENTS

Most of the photographs are from the collections of Bristol Museums & Art Gallery. The photographs on page 109 are reproduced by kind permission of Avon & Somerset Constabulary. I am grateful to my colleagues at Bristol Museums & Art Gallery for their support, and particularly to Paul Elkin and Andy King; special thanks are due to Francis Greenacre who made many useful suggestions to the text. I am also grateful to the staff of the Bristol Record Office for permission to reproduce the photographs on page 8, 18 top, 27, 72 top, 73 top, 79, 84 bottom, 95 top, 98 top, and especially to Alison Brown who helped identify Thomas Denford and George King in the photographs.

Primary sources used included parliamentary reports into sanitary conditions in 1845 and manufactures in 1866, local newspapers, trade directories, census returns, building plan records; port records and the Fry's business archive in the BRO. There is a huge literature on Bristol and many published books and articles were consulted: below is a brief list of those which proved to be invaluable in preparing this book.

Anderson, C., *A City and its Cinemas*, Redcliffe, 1983

Bettey, J.H., *Bristol Observed*, Redcliffe, 1986

Bishop, I.S., *The City & Kingswood Line, A History of Bristol's Trams*, Bishop, 1995

Cohen, L., *Greater Bristol by Lesser Columbus*, Pelham Press, 1893

Crick, C., *Victorian Buildings in Bristol*, Redcliffe, 1975

Dresser, M. & Ollenshaw, P., *The Making of Modern Bristol*, Redcliffe, 1996

Elkin, P., *Images of Maritime Bristol*, Breedon, 1995

Harvey, C. & Press, J., *Studies in the Business History of Bristol*, Bristol Academic Press, 1988

Jones, D., *A History of Clifton*, Phillimore, 1992

Latimer, J., *Annals of Bristol, Nineteenth Century, 1887*, reprinted Kingsmead, 1970

Little, B., *The Story of Bristol*, Redcliffe, 1991

Mallory, K., *The Bristol House*, Redcliffe, 1985

Mellor, H.E., *Leisure and the Changing City*, Routledge & Kegan Paul, 1976

Stone, G.F., *Bristol As It Was – And As It Is*, Walter Reid, 1909

Wells, C., & Stone, G.F., *Bristol and the Great War*, Arrowsmith, 1920

White, G., *Tramlines to the Stars*, Redcliffe, 1995

Many of the pamphlets published by the Bristol Branch of the Historical Association were also valuable sources of information and the many photograph compilations by Reece Winstone were also useful.

Part Two
Bristol 1920–1969

Park Street from the Art Gallery, *c.* 1950. One of the principal shopping streets in the city, Park Street was badly damaged during the blitz and at the time of this view there were still several large gaps in the street. They were later filled, however, with façades matching the original buildings. The bus advertising George's beers is on its way to Henbury and is painted in the new post-war green livery. In the distance the CWS building and the Royal Hotel stand out against the city centre haze, while the presence of the City Docks is marked by several cranes.

INTRODUCTION

A nother book of old photographs of Bristol? My initial response was surely there will be little demand, when the idea of a title in Sutton Publishing's *Britain in Old Photographs* series was first suggested. Over forty volumes of Reece Winstone's books, plus a large number of other works, has resulted in a strong photographic record of Bristol in print. Nevertheless, the book went ahead. The original idea was to cover the hundred years from 1850 to 1950 but it soon became clear that there was sufficient material for two books, and so the first was published in 1996 under the title *Bristol 1850–1919*. The book concentrated on Bristol's expansion and modernisation in Victorian and Edwardian times, concluding with a section on the city's contribution to the First World War.

This second volume continues the record from 1920, beyond 1950, to 1969. This fifty-year period effectively covers the mid-twentieth century, and while many previous books on Bristol have split this into three separate periods (the inter-war years of the 1920s and 1930s, the Second World War from 1939 to 1945 and the post-war era, particularly concentrating on the city in the 1950s), I have chosen to group these together in order to emphasise continuity in the city's development between the 1920s and 1960s. However, the book is not organised chronologically and does not attempt a 'blow-by-blow' account of the city in this period. Instead, the photographs are arranged thematically into eight sections looking at the port, trade and industry, the city centre, retailing, home life, leisure, local government and services and the Second World War. The impact of the war (throughout the text 'the war' refers exclusively to the Second World War, 1939–45) is evident in virtually every aspect of life in the city but the photographs in the final section convey something of the awfulness of life in war-time Bristol.

Enemy bombing wrought terrible damage to the centre of Bristol and the inner suburbs – parts of Bedminster, for example, suffered badly; but this was only one of several major factors affecting the development of mid-twentieth century Bristol. Greater involvement of government – central and local – in town planning and the provision of services and amenities played a major part in shaping the city in this period. In particular, the City Council tightened its hold on the overall development of Bristol:

regional plans made jointly with Bath and other neighbouring urban districts were first drawn up in 1925 and continued to be produced through the 1930s – but they were only advisory; it was the 1947 Town & Country Planning Act which transformed the City Council's role from one of mere regulation to active control of the city's development. Henceforward, the city planners' vision for Bristol was backed by law and so the city's first Development Plan published in 1952 had a major bearing on the city's development until the late 1960s – not only because of the breadth of its scope, but because it defined the city's chief priorities: the building of new homes and schools and the control of traffic.

The provision of housing by the Council – which became mandatory after 1919 – was an area where the local authority made a conspicuous contribution to the development of the city in this period and one which radically altered the lives of thousands of people. By the 1960s roughly 40 per cent of Bristol's population lived in council houses which set new standards of accommodation. The mid-twentieth century saw a general rise in the standard of living with particularly marked rises in the 1930s and 1950s; it was in the 1930s that home ownership first became a major national trend and in Bristol (as elsewhere) this was represented by the building of many thousands of private houses. The 1930s also saw electricity supplies reach most homes and the acquisition of the first electric domestic appliances, while the 1950s and 1960s saw a revolution in levels of expectation for most people, with an even wider level of ownership of domestic and personal consumer goods, including electric washing machines, television sets and motor cars. The levels of comfort and convenience in the home – and the time available for leisure – were a world apart from the Bristol of 1920.

Motorised traffic has played a major part in shaping the development of the city since the end of the First World War. In 1920, apart from taxis and trams owned by the Bristol Tramways & Carriage Company – and thousands of bicycles – most of the traffic on the roads was horse drawn. Car ownership was a luxury restricted to the wealthy. But the 1920s saw a rapid increase in private motor cars while horse-drawn carts and wagons began to give way to motorised vans and lorries. The consequences were enormous: new words entered everyday language – motorists, car parks and petrol stations – while the numbers of wheelwrights, farriers and saddlers dwindled to be replaced by motor garages and car mechanics. Most important of all was the increase in the volume of traffic on the streets. There were several issues here, of which safety was one: the early 1930s saw the introduction of traffic lights and belisha beacons to better control junctions and make road crossings safer for pedestrians; motorists began to demand car parks; and, most critically, the extra traffic caused congestion. From the 1930s city planners became increasingly preoccupied with easing and regulating traffic flow through the city, and from then until the 1960s many drastic changes were wrought to the fabric of the city in the name of the motor car.

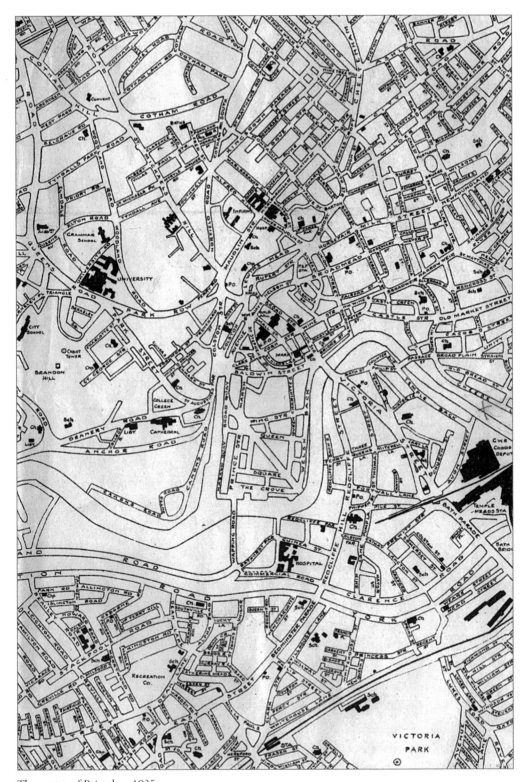

The centre of Bristol, *c.* 1935.

The car and motor bus gave people unprecedented freedom and this was a factor in the expansion of the city. Bristol continued to push out its boundaries into the surrounding countryside: north-westwards to include much of Henbury and the Severnside industrial district and southwards to Withywood, Hengrove and Stockwood. The total acreage of the city increased from 18,436 acres in 1920 to 27,068 acres by 1969. The population also increased, although not as dramatically as the period 1850–1919. In 1920 the population of Bristol was 376,975, reaching a peak of 445,000 in 1955. Thereafter it started to drop, as old housing in the inner city was cleared and because people moved beyond the city boundaries to new urban areas such as Nailsea and Yate. Mid-twentieth-century Bristol, therefore, while a third larger than its Victorian and Edwardian predecessor, was less densely populated.

Searching for the photographs has been an enjoyable, though at times frustrating, exercise: while some subjects are well represented in the photographic record – there is no shortage of photographs of the city centre, for example – other subjects proved elusive and so photographs alone cannot represent every facet of life in the city. The objective, nevertheless, was to make a selection which shows something of the diversity of life in the city, to catch the mood and atmosphere of mid-twentieth-century Bristol and to emphasise the pace of change in this period. For architectural variety, compare the striking modernistic Odeon and showrooms of 1938 (see p. 188) with the timber-framed house in King Street (see p. 187); for contrasts in living conditions over time, compare the scullery of the house in Old Quarry Road – typical of the 1920s – (see p. 239) with the modern all-electric laundry in the council block in 1960. For mood, the group of photographs taken on a council estate in about 1947 convey the optimism of post-war reconstruction, the 'brave new world' that was being forged out of austerity (see pp. 244–45). The photographs also show some well-known buildings such as the Dutch House, a victim of the blitz in 1940 (see p. 185), and the Shot Tower on Redcliff Hill (see p. 159), a victim of a 1960s road-widening scheme; these remind us of the many changes which have taken place in the city between 1920 and 1969.

CHAPTER TEN

THE PORT & DOCKS

Ships and Bristol, as everyone knows, are inseparable. Bristol's early development was based on sea-borne trade, and over the centuries the port has exerted a huge influence over the city's economy, its physical character and identity. Until the last century much of the city's industrial and commercial life has revolved around the port: major industries such as soap making, leather working, tobacco and chocolate manufacture relied upon raw materials brought in by sea, while many other trades and industries – boat and ship building, sail making, rope making and coopering, for example – developed as an adjunct to the port. The city's arms depict a ship and Bristol Castle, reflecting the strong physical presence of the port in the heart of the city. When the Floating Harbour was created in 1809 by damming up the course of the Avon, some 86 acres of deep water were formed between the western entrance at the Cumberland Basin and Temple Meads to the east, while an arm of the docks – St Augustine's Reach – penetrated the city centre. Here was the 'street of ships' in a unique city landscape where cranes and warehouses rubbed shoulders with fashionable shops, offices and old parish churches. Throughout this period working ships remained an everyday sight in the City Docks – as the photographs show – but they were, nevertheless, in slow decline and the number of ships using the Floating Harbour fell rapidly in the late 1960s and early 1970s.

By the 1920s Bristol's position as one of the country's leading ports was based on the docks at Avonmouth and Portishead. These had been built in the 1870s by separate companies – in competition with each other and the Corporation-owned City Docks – to attract the larger ships of the second half of the nineteenth century, which were unable to negotiate the tortuous journey up the Avon to the city or even be accommodated in the Floating Harbour. In 1884 they were taken over by the City Corporation and in 1926 a new committee, the Port of Bristol Authority, was created to run all three dock sites. Although Avonmouth had been absorbed within the city boundaries in 1904, the docks 'down the mouth' at Avonmouth and Portishead existed as exclusive dock environments. They were out of sight save for those who worked in them, and never captured the imagination of Bristolians and visitors as did the old City Docks.

Avonmouth Docks had been greatly enlarged in 1908 by the opening of the Royal Edward Dock, connected to the original dock of 1877 by a junction cut, and it was here rather than at Portishead that much of the subsequent expansion of the port occurred. The opening of this dock capable of taking any ship then afloat enabled the port to develop trade from beyond its traditional links with Africa and across the Atlantic to new partners particularly in the Far East. In 1921 the Royal Edward Dock was enlarged by a western extension, followed by an eastern arm extension opened in 1928 and further extended between 1939 and 1945. A conspicuous feature of the Royal Edward Dock was the huge dry dock, 875 ft long, where ships could be brought in for repairs and maintenance. This graving dock remained a useful facility throughout the mid-twentieth century, and in 1969 was still the largest in the Bristol Channel.

The volume of trade handled by the port steadily increased between 1920 and 1969 rising from an annual net tonnage of about 2½ million tons in 1920 to just under 8 million tons by 1969. Imported goods far outweighed the value and tonnage of exports: in 1934 exports were 41,463 tons compared to imports of 2,335,460 tons, and although exports – notably of motor cars – increased after the war, rising to roughly 200,000 tons by 1969, they still represented a small percentage of the total goods handled by the port. Throughout this period general cargoes formed an important part of the port's trade, but it was the importation of several important bulk cargoes which dominated in terms of tonnage, value and also in terms of their impact on the dock landscape. Grain and timber were two of these: the former a relatively new trade dating to the second half of the nineteenth century when cheap North American wheat flooded the market, while the import of timber was an old-established trade dating to the late middle ages. Up to 1939 some of the shipments of these two cargoes still arrived on large sailing vessels. By the 1920s grain was one of the port's principal imports and continued to rise in this period: by 1969 roughly one million tons of grain were being shipped into the port – about an eighth of the net tonnage of imports. Grains imported included wheat from North America, maize from North and South America and the Black Sea, and barley from North Africa, Canada and the Black Sea. Granaries and mills were prominent features of the docks in the City Docks and at Avonmouth where the number of granaries increased from two in the early 1920s to five by 1965. After the war grain storage and milling was increasingly concentrated at Avonmouth, and the port's 1954 guide claimed that Avonmouth was the most important centre for milling in the south-west. Timber was unloaded at all three docks, where large stacks of timber piled in extensive yards were prominent features. Softwood for the building trade continued to be shipped in huge quantities from the Baltic and North America, while tropical hardwoods were brought from Africa and the Far East. By 1969, however, the trade in timber was showing signs of decline.

In contrast, the importation of petroleum was a relatively new trade and one that grew steadily throughout this period. In 1902 imports of petroleum were a mere 75,793 tons, but by 1934 had exceeded 600,000 tons and by 1969 had risen to 3,000,000 tons. Oil tankers were berthed in the Oil Basin at the Royal Edward Dock where an extensive system of pipelines connected with the storage tanks, which increased considerably in numbers between 1920 and 1969. Large quantities of zinc concentrates (which contain sulphur) unloaded at Avonmouth went straight to the National Smelting Co.'s works established after the First World War alongside the Royal Edward Dock, where they were processed into zinc and sulphuric acid. Similarly, Bristol's important paper-making, packaging and printing industry was supplied with wood pulp, paper and newsprint.

Imports of food and drink were also important and sustained some well-known and long-established Bristol industries such as tobacco, which continued to provide major business for the port. In the 1920s annual imports of tobacco stood at 20,000 tons – about 25 per cent of the UK total – and by 1969 had risen to 32,000 tons. Between 1905 and 1919 three bonded tobacco warehouses were built by the Corporation at Cumberland Basin, and in the mid-1920s further bonded warehouses of startling white concrete were built overlooking the Floating Harbour at Canon's Marsh and at Winterstoke Road, Ashton, by the Imperial Tobacco Group. The increase in imports of cocoa – supplying the industry at Bournville as well as in Bristol – was dramatic, from 15,881 tons in 1934 to a record total of 49,182 tons in 1969. In the nineteenth century Bristol merchants trading with West Africa – such as the Lucas Brothers (see *Bristol 1850–1919*, page 41) – maintained their own fleets of ships; by the 1930s, however, the port's service with West Africa was in the hands of the Elder Dempster Line. Tea imports also rose, particularly after the Second World War, and by 1969 over half the tea drunk in Britain was passing through the port. Wine and sherry imports again date to the early history of the port. In the 1930s Bristol remained the chief English port for the importation of wine; added to the traditional links with Portugal and Spain, the port had successfully built up business with wine from the Empire.

In the 1930s steamers of the Isthmian Line unloaded canned fruit and fish from San Francisco and other Pacific ports, while vessels of the Federal, Shaw, New Zealand Shipping Co., Commonwealth and Dominion Lines, Shaw and Clan Line imported meat and dairy produce from New Zealand and Australia. The 1928 extension at the Royal Edward Dock included a cold store for the storage of meat and dairy produce to cater for the expanding trade with New Zealand and Australia. Another important trade in the period covered here was the banana trade, which had only begun in 1901 when the first shipment of bananas from Jamaica was unloaded at Avonmouth. In 1912 the part-American-owned Elders & Fyffes line took over the trade, and for over fifty years their distinctive white steam ships with buff funnels – which also carried mail and passengers between Avonmouth and the West Indies – were a familiar sight at Avonmouth. In the 1930s a third of all bananas brought into England were handled at Avonmouth, and it was a heavy blow to the port when Elders & Fyffes transferred the trade to Southampton in 1967.

The passenger service with the West Indies operated by Elders & Fyffes was only one of several ocean passenger services which operated from the port in the 1920s and 1930s. There were sailings to Rangoon on ships of the Henderson and Bibby Lines and to Australia and New Zealand by Bethell, Gwyn & Co.'s lines. The Royal Edward Dock had a passenger station and special trains connected with arriving and departing liners and mainline railway services. There were also services to other British and European ports, although the volume of passenger traffic fell sharply after the war.

Throughout this period the handling of a wide variety of miscellaneous commodities – the port called them general cargoes – remained important, and in 1969 accounted for over one million tons of imports. For their swift dispatch transit sheds were introduced toward the end of the nineteenth century on the quaysides at Avonmouth and in the City Docks. At Canon's Marsh and Dean's Marsh in the city some of the transit sheds were fitted with 2-ton electric cranes mounted on the roof which were capable of unloading cargoes directly from ship's holds. Other sheds were served by tall electric cranes on the quayside, such as those installed in 1951 in front of L & M sheds on Princes Wharf, built on the site of the corporation granary which had been bombed in 1941. Four of these cranes built by Stothert & Pitt of Bath are now preserved *in situ* on their 15 ft gauge track outside L and M sheds now occupied by the Bristol Industrial Museum; together, the sheds, cranes, railway track and other items of quayside furniture preserve a section of the distinctive dock environment within view of the city centre.

Other mechanical handling equipment such as electrically powered hoists, trolleys and trucks was introduced after the First World War, but the movement of many cargoes in the docks still relied heavily on human muscle. The unloading of Jamaican bananas, for example, in spite of the aid of elevators, still required the labour of some 300 men. Thus a large workforce of dockers and stevedores found employment in the docks: in the 1920s there were about 3,000 dockers employed in Bristol. Dockers were general labourers, while stevedores were employed loading and unloading ships. The work was hard, repetitive and dangerous: accidents were common and employment was uncertain. The arrival of a banana boat was regarded as a 'plum' job guaranteeing three days' work, but at other times this large, casual workforce would stand idle waiting for work. In 1922 the Transport & General Workers' Union was founded under the leadership of Ernest Bevin (1881–1951), a Bristol carter who had become a full-time official of the Dock, Wharf, Riverside and General Workers' Union in 1911. The Union sought to decasualise the work, a conflict which remained unresolved until 1967

Canon's Road, 1920s. Originally entitled 'Winter's Golden Ray', this photograph shows motor lorries, horse-drawn traffic and a lone cyclist on the granite sets in Canon's Road. The back of W transit shed on Dean's Marsh is on the left with U and V sheds further back; the City Lead Works of Rowe Brothers & Co. is on the right. They started business in about 1884 as manufacturers of plumbers' goods, but by the inter-war period were selling a wide range of domestic hardware from their showrooms in Victoria Street.

when dockers found security under the 'Jobs for Life' labour agreement. The increase in containerised cargoes, however, in the 1960s allowed for greater mechanical handling, and the sight of quaysides teeming with dockers manhandling goods between ships and road and rail vehicles became increasingly rare.

Railways were another important part of the dock environment. The port served an extensive hinterland reaching as far as the Midlands, the entire south-west, as well as South Wales. Goods to and from the docks were moved via the Severn navigation to the Midlands and by coastal shipping to other ports in England and South Wales, but the railways formed the chief means of bulk long-distance transport for much of this period. The first rail connection with the docks was made in 1872 when the Great Western and Bristol & Exeter railways jointly opened a Bristol Harbour line from Temple Meads through Redcliff to Princes Wharf. In 1906 a new connection to the docks was opened, which left the Portishead line at Ashton Gate and then crossed the New Cut on the bottom of a new, hydraulically operated, double-deck swing bridge. The line then split, one route running beside the New Cut to connect with the existing track at Princes Wharf, while the second crossed the Cumberland Basin by another swing bridge and then continued alongside Hotwells Road, past the gas works, to a new goods depot at Canon's Marsh.

Both the docks at Avonmouth and Portishead had rail connections from the start. The Portishead line actually predated the opening of the docks, having opened in 1867, while the Midland Railway joined forces with the Great Western to create a new route to Avonmouth in time for the opening of the dock in 1877. In the early 1900s the Great Western Railway made further connections between Avonmouth and its main line to South Wales at Patchway and with its route to the Midlands at Filton. The Port Authority's 1935 Guide claimed that all ship's berths, transit sheds, warehouses, granaries and cold stores were served by its own railway lines, which connected with those of the Great Western and London Midland & Scottish Railway. However, competition from road transport gradually increased during this period. In 1926, with the opening of the four-lane Portway, the docks at Avonmouth acquired a direct road link with Bristol and further afield, and this encouraged a switch to the movement of goods to and from the port by motor lorry. From the 1960s the shift to road haulage, especially upon the opening of the M4 and M5 motorways in stages from the mid-1960s, caused a major decline – as elsewhere – in the use of the railways, and by 1969 the quayside railways at Portishead and Avonmouth were little used. In the City Docks much of the network closed in 1964 and 1965, leaving just the section between Ashton Junction and Wapping Wharf. This continued in use for coal traffic until 1986 and now survives as the preserved Bristol Harbour Railway, which operates two Bristol-built dock shunting locomotives formerly owned by the Port Authority.

The closure of the railway lines around the City Docks was, of course, just one part of their decline which had accelerated after the war. In 1946 Charles Hill & Sons' Bristol City Line transferred from the city to Avonmouth Docks, to enable it to operate larger ships and remain competitive on the trans-Atlantic route. By 1951, 90 per cent of the port's trade went through Avonmouth yet the City Docks remained busy, receiving general cargoes coastwise and from the continent. But in the 1960s coastal shipping declined sharply in the face of competition from motorway-borne road haulage and continental traffic, such as the importation of wood pulp, was transferred to the rivermouth docks. It was clear that the City Docks were no longer commercially viable, and in 1969 the City Council applied for an Act to close the City Docks to sea-going traffic; this was obtained the following year. From the late 1960s the number of working ships entering the Floating Harbour declined rapidly. The timber trade finally left the old docks in 1973 and Charles Hill launched their last ship – the *Miranda Guinness* – in 1976. For another thirteen years sand dredgers and the Wessex Water sludge ship – the *Glen Avon* – kept alive the memory of working ships in the City Docks, but they had gone by 1990. Meanwhile, in an age of much reduced global seaborne trade, the port continued to modernise and adapt to new trends, and the 1960s saw the planning of a new dock at the mouth of the Avon – the West Dock – soon to become better known as the Royal Portbury Dock, which opened in 1978.

Junction Lock Bridge, Cumberland Basin, *c.* 1935. Contrasting forms of road transport cross Junction Lock, which provides access from the Cumberland Basin to the Floating Harbour. The lock was designed by Thomas Howard, the Docks Engineer, and built in 1871. The present bridge was built in 1925 by William Cowlin & Son, Bristol's leading construction company, with the steel construction by John Lysaght & Sons of the Netham Iron Works, Bristol. Cowlin's were also responsible for the three massive red brick bonded warehouses which dominate the western end of the docks. These were built by the City Corporation to store imported tobacco in secure bonded warehouses, where the tobacco was kept under the care of Customs & Excise authorities until required for use. The duty was paid when the tobacco was released for manufacture. The earliest, A Bond, visible behind the bus, was built in 1905 and incorporates a combined steel and cast-iron frame encased in brickwork. B Bond, to the right, was built two years later, and while externally very similar is structurally quite different, being built by the Coignet system of reinforced concrete. The Nova Scotia Hotel beyond the bridge dates to about 1811, and the name may relate to the former maritime trade between Bristol and Nova Scotia. The Cumberland Basin contained a landing stage for livestock shipped from Ireland, which was just beyond the railings on the right, and from here the cattle were taken across the road to the lairs and slaughter houses behind the wall on the extreme left; these remained in use until the 1950s and now the area is occupied by housing built in about 1980.

Horse-drawn traffic was still a common sight on roads in the 1930s, although in sharp decline. Approaching the camera is a lightweight commercial wagon drawn by a pony. The double-decker bus was to become a familiar part of the street scene in Bristol (as in other towns and cities) during the rest of the twentieth century, but at the time this photograph was taken was still a relatively novel sight. Apart from a short-lived experiment with double-decker buses in 1908–9, the Bristol Tramways & Carriage Company relied on single-deck buses until the introduction of the G-type model in 1931. This particular example entered service in 1932 and is seen in the dark blue and white livery of the BT & CC, which lasted until the Second World War.

Bridge swing at Junction Lock, 11 August 1961. The Ashton swing bridge was last opened in 1934, but the frequent opening of the Junction Lock bridge caused traffic congestion on this principal route to the south-west. Here, holiday traffic is held up by a bridge swing as the *Manja Dan*, a Danish vessel of the Lauritzen line, leaves the docks on her way to Bordeaux. The ship had arrived from Kotka, Finland, two days earlier with a cargo of paper, wood pulp, newsprint, plywood and blockboard. These vessels, with their bright red hulls and cream upper decks, were a familiar sight in the City Docks at this time.

View across the Cumberland Basin to Hotwells and Clifton, 1930s. A boy with a cart made from a Sunlight soap box looks over to houses in Hotwells, demolished in 1963 when the elevated roads leading to the Plimsoll Bridge were built. The boy is standing beside the original lock connecting the Cumberland Basin with the Floating Harbour which passed close to the Nova Scotia public house, behind the photographer. The lock was replaced by the present Junction Lock in about 1871 and blocked off.

Cumberland Basin and the New Cut, *c.* 1963. All three tobacco bonded warehouses are seen in this aerial view of the western approach to the City Docks: C Bond on the left and A and B Bond in the centre of the view. The Cumberland Basin, the entrance to the Floating Harbour, is to the right, while the New Cut, which carries the tidal waters of the Avon south of the docks is in the centre of the view: happily, this photograph was taken at high tide, as at low water the muddy banks of the cut and river beyond present a less attractive picture! The chimney visible centre right marks the location of the Underfall Yard, the headquarters and workshops of the Docks Engineer's department. The chimney is part of the hydraulic pumping station built in 1888 to provide power to operate the swing bridges and lock gates of the Cumberland Basin.

The photograph records the western end of the Docks shortly before the scene was dramatically transformed by the building of the Cumberland road system, designed to ease traffic congestion on the busy route to the south-west. Previously all traffic leaving the city had to cross the Cumberland Basin by the Junction Lock Bridge before crossing the upper deck of the Ashton Swing Bridge. Traffic congestion was particularly bad when the Junction Lock Bridge was swung to allow ships to travel between the Cumberland Basin, top right, and the main part of the Floating Harbour. Preparations for construction of the new road network, designed by the City Engineer's Department, are evident in this view: buildings have been cleared in Hotwells to make way for the new approach roads to the Plimsoll Bridge which crosses the Cumberland Basin and the New Cut; the foundations of the Fixed crossing at the mouth of the New Cut appear to be in place; and a crane can be seen to the left of B Bond, the westernmost of the three tobacco warehouses.

The Plimsoll Bridge was opened in April 1965 and the upper deck of the Ashton Swing Bridge and the embankment leading to it were removed. In spite of the many slip roads and flyovers designed to keep traffic moving, the Cumberland Basin road system remains a traffic black-spot, and motorists from the Portishead direction negotiating the difficult crossing towards Ashton must wonder if this particular link was overlooked by the designers! Junction Lock Bridge remains in use to connect Hotwells Road with Cumberland Road, and the lower deck of the Ashton Swing Bridge which carried the railway line from Ashton Junction to Canon's Marsh and Wapping Wharf was retained and remains in limited use today by steam trains operated by the Bristol Harbour Railway. The railway line to Canon's Marsh was closed in 1965, and the bridge carrying the single track line across the eastern end of the Junction Lock was removed.

View from Brandon Hill of the Canon's Marsh gasworks, *c.* 1950. The gasworks at Canon's Marsh was established in 1823, originally manufacturing gas from whale and seal oil and subsequently coal gas; it ceased production in the 1950s. On the other side of the docks lines of railway trucks can be seen on Wapping Wharf, while beyond lie the densely packed streets of Southville and Bedminster.

City Docks, 26 July 1958. Five large ships are visible in this view. Berthed at Canon's Marsh alongside Y and Z sheds is the *Kamma Dan* of the Lauritzen line, which has probably unloaded a shipment of wood pulp. On the right the Norwegian vessel the *Stalheim* is being towed towards the Cumberland basin by the tug, *John King*, now preserved at the Bristol Industrial Museum; carrying general cargo, the *Stalheim* was on her way to Oslo via Newport. Behind the transit sheds the tobacco bonds built in the 1920s and demolished in 1989 are visible.

St Augustine's Reach, 30 April 1958. Scenes of docking and cargo handling continued to be visible from the city centre into the 1960s, although the quaysides were out of bounds to the general public. Here, timber is being unloaded from the *Crane* on to lorries using one of the roof cranes fitted to U and V sheds. The *Crane* had arrived the previous day from Bordeaux and Tornnay-Charente, carrying wine and brandy and other miscellaneous goods. The vessel left the following day for Dublin before returning to Bordeaux.

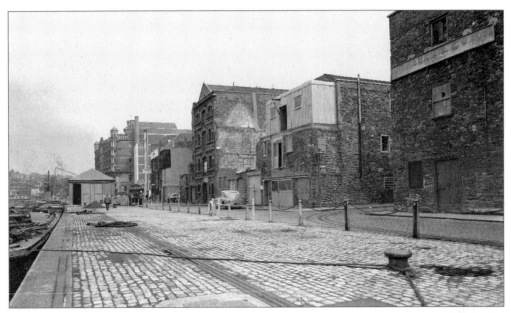

Narrow Quay, 11 August 1961. Old warehouses fronting the quay were soon to come down to make way for a new hotel and multi-storey car park. The Co-operative and Wholesale building of 1906 beyond the warehouses survived for another decade before being demolished to make way for Broad Quay House. The granite sets of the quayside survive, however.

St Augustine's Reach, August 1947. Scandinavian wood pulp is being unloaded into road vehicles and lighters from the Swedish ship, the *Inger*, at U shed using the roof-mounted cranes. The lighters – or barges – will carry the pulp up river to the St Anne's Board Mills; they remained an essential part of the City Docks until the 1960s. The *Inger* arrived in the City Docks from Sweden on 24 August 1947, and after 1,500 tons of wood pulp had been unloaded it sailed for Preston on 30 August.

The Bristol Harbour railway, looking towards Temple Meads from the roof of St Mary Redcliffe, c. 1950. Opened in 1872, this was the first railway connection with the City Docks, starting from Temple Meads on a brick viaduct before entering a tunnel beneath the churchyard of St Mary Redcliffe and then crossing the Bathurst Basin on a steam-operated bascule (lifting) bridge. Redcliff goods yard, seen here, once handled a large amount of flour and coal traffic but closed in 1962, and closure of the line followed in January 1964.

Advertisement for Coast Lines Limited, 1935. In the mid-1930s Coast Line steamers maintained three services a week from Liverpool and weekly from London, Manchester, Penzance, Aberdeen and other ports. They continued to trade from the City Docks until the 1960s.

Aerial view of Avonmouth Docks, *c.* 1965. By 1920 the greater part of the Port of Bristol's trade was concentrated at Avonmouth; its importance was reflected in the extensions built by the Port Authority in the 1920s and the extensive industrial development which occurred beside the docks. The photograph shows the original dock of 1877 on the right and, in the centre, the junction cut which connected to the much larger Royal Edward Dock of 1908, which was enlarged by the western and eastern arm extensions opened in 1921 and 1928 respectively.

Royal Edward Dock, Avonmouth, 30 June 1954. A general view of the dock showing *Birmingham City* of the Bristol City line at R Berth on the left, *Kent* at O Berth in the centre of the view and in the distance *Florence Holt*, moored alongside a cluster of cranes at T Berth, which is to the right of the main entrance to the docks and immediately to the right of the entrance to the graving dock.

The Blue Funnel liner *Calchas* at S Berth, Royal Edward Dock, Avonmouth, 28 April 1954. Development of trade with the Far East was an important aspect of the port's twentieth-century expansion. The *Calchas* had just arrived from the Far East loaded with timber and a general cargo including pineapples; she left two days later for Swansea. In 1969 Blue Funnel were still advertising fast monthly sailings from the Far East to Avonmouth.

Cuban sugar being discharged from the *Chamois* directly to road and rail vehicles at Avonmouth, 17 June 1953. The railway wagons belong to the Port Authority. The *Chamois* had arrived from Havana on 14 June and left for Quebec on 25 June.

A 1960s view of the west side of the Eastern Arm extension of the Royal Edward Dock, built in 1928 and modernised in the late 1950s and 1960s with new cranes and other bulk-handling equipment. The railway system was also revised to provide a more flexible system, enabling movement of trains of wagons to suit several vessels at different stages of loading or discharging. In this view timber is being unloaded on to flat railway trucks and lorries.

Dockers at Avonmouth Docks handling sacks, 1930s. Goods such as rice, bran, sugar and animal feed arrived at the por in hessian sacks and were unloaded by a casual workforce of dockers and stevedores. Hard toil and uncertain employment were the lot of dockers for most of this period; they were tough, hard men possessed of great physical strength. The adoption of containerisation of loads and the increased use of mechanical handling in the 1960s reduced the demand for large labour force at the very time that dockers won security of employment.

CHAPTER ELEVEN

TRADE & INDUSTRY

I n 1933 J.B. Priestley found Bristol a lively, bustling city, 'earning its living and spending its own money . . . achieving a new prosperity by selling us Gold Flake and Fry's chocolate and soap and clothes and a hundred other things'. The range of Bristol industries was indeed quite remarkable and rooted in the city's early medieval origins, when the woollen industry, soap manufacture, ship building and a wide range of wood, leather and metal trades were sustained by maritime trade. Raw materials, essential for many of the city's industries, were brought in by sea: tallow, leather hides, metals and metal ores, cocoa beans, tobacco leaf and wines and sherry. The variety of industrial activity in the city was further stimulated by Bristol's pre-eminence in the south-west: Bristol traditionally dominated trade over much of the region, and as one of the largest cities in the country (seventh largest in 1940) it contained a large urban market stimulating a demand for almost everything.

In 1940 the Bristol Development Board claimed that there were 2,248 factories and workshops in Bristol representing some 300 different industries. A few of these dominated the city, the manufacture of tobacco products, for example, and chocolate, which made the name Bristol famous world wide. In 1928 the City Council's publication *Bristol Commercially Considered* stated that there were 11,000 people employed in the food, drink and tobacco industries; the paper and printing trades employed nearly as many, accounting for 9,000 jobs in the city; while engineering and allied trades provided 13,592 jobs. The larger factories belonging to companies such as W.D. & H.O. Wills formed major city landmarks. The Wills factories on East Street and Raleigh Road in Bedminster towered over the neighbouring streets of terraced houses. Until they relocated to Keynsham, Fry's factories, eight of them in total, dominated a cramped site around the Pithay, and their factory chimneys were as conspicuous a city-centre landmark as the nearby church towers. There were several other large works in or close to the centre: breweries, flour mills on Redcliffe Back, an electricity generating station (belonging to the Bristol Tramway & Carriage Company) and Llewellin & James's brass foundry on Castle Green. East of the centre at Broad Plain was the impressive factory of Christopher Thomas & Brothers, soap and candle makers, modelled on a Florentine palace, and next to it the Midland Iron Works of Gardiner Sons & Co.; they specialised in the manufacture of architectural iron and brasswork which adorned many important shops, offices and public buildings in the city.

Many other major industries were located in the eastern districts of the city. Beyond Temple Meads barges carried raw materials up river to Barton Hill and St Philip's Marsh, lying either side of the Feeder Canal, where chemical works, glue and paint factories, potteries, gas works and railway engine sheds filled the air with smoke. Barges carried wood pulp transferred from foreign vessels in the City Docks to the large board mills at St Anne's, established in 1912 by Imperial Tobacco, where it was converted into cardboard packaging for tobacco, chocolates, cereals and other foodstuffs. At Crew's Hole there were more chemical works, while south of the Avon at Brislington the Bristol Tramways and Carriage Company had their works for bus construction. The spread of industry continued eastwards beyond the city's boundaries into Kingswood and Hanham in Gloucestershire, where clothing, footwear and brushmaking were carried on: the Kleen-e-ze Brush Company started the manufacture of brushes in Hanham in the 1920s. In the early twentieth century Fishponds became established as a new engineering centre of Bristol.

While the larger firms dominated the local economy there were also many smaller workshop-based industries and trades employing skilled labour: typically these were small family concerns chiefly making household and personal consumer goods. Some had quite a rural flavour and perpetuated traditional handcrafts, for example basket makers or saddlers, such as Shattock & Hunter in Frogmore Street. Until 1953 S. Sale & Sons continued to make clogs in West Street: these were worn by workers at George's brewery, Fry's and other local factories. The making of shoes and leather trunks were two other important leather trades; there were also hatters, tailors and dressmakers and wood and furniture trades including upholstery. Many small businesses were found in or close to the city centre: thus furniture makers and upholsterers were concentrated in St Pauls.

As it didn't rely too heavily on one particular industry, Bristol's economy proved resilient in difficult times such as the early 1920s, when trade was disrupted following the end of the First World War. Bristol also escaped the worst effects of the depression of the early 1930s, although the city did suffer hardship: unemployment reached 10 per cent in these years, and in February 1932 a march by 10,000 demonstrators protesting against unemployment flared into violence in Old Market, and thirty people were injured. The 1920s saw the demise of several formerly important industries. The last glass cones in the city – at Powell and Ricketts bottle works in Avon Street – were fired for the final time in 1923, and in 1925 the Great Western Cotton Works, which had been a major source of employment in Barton Hill since 1838, closed. Coal mining had been in steady decline in the city since the late nineteenth century and the last collieries in the city closed around this time; with them went the brickworks which had used the clay found with the coal seams. The clothing trades contracted from the 1920s, while the footwear industry – one of the largest employers in the early twentieth century – suffered a major decline between 1920 and 1969. Other old-established industries, however, continued to thrive, and there were many firms, such as Fry's, Harvey's and Wills, which had been in business in the city since the eighteenth century. Lead shot continued to be made using the tower on Redcliff Hill that William Watts, the inventor of the process, had built in about 1782. Ferris & Co., manufacturers of pharmaceutical products in Union Street, had been established in 1754, and E.A. & W. Greenslade, brush and plane manufacturers, in 1727.

By the 1920s several new industries were emerging which were to become vital to the city's prosperity in the mid-twentieth century. Most spectacular was the expansion of the aircraft industry following the creation of the British and Colonial Aeroplane Company at Filton by Sir George White in 1910. In 1920 the company changed its name to the Bristol Aeroplane Company, and alongside the manufacture of aeroplanes began the production of aero-engines. After a period of retrenchment up to 1934 production increased in response to the government's rearmament programme, which placed a strong emphasis on air power, and by 1939 the company was the largest single employer in the city, providing jobs to over 18,000 people. During the war the company manufactured the Blenheim, the Beaufighter and other military aircraft and also produced 101,000 engines. After the war the company developed the Bristol Brabazon as a long-haul passenger aircraft. The prototype made its maiden flight in 1949 among much local optimism: at the time this handsome eight-engined aircraft was the largest passenger aircraft in the world. The optimism, sadly, was misplaced and even before a second prototype could be completed it was evident that the future lay with jet airliners; the project was abandoned and the Brabazon scrapped. The Britannia, another graceful aeroplane, soon followed. Powered by four turboprop engines, it enjoyed limited success, but it was the small, ugly, but useful Bristol Freighter which brought commercial success to the company in the field of civil aviation in the 1950s. By the late 1950s it was apparent that the day of the independent aircraft manufacturer was over, and the Bristol Aeroplane Company merged with other leading manufacturers to form the British Aircraft Corporation; in the 1960s the aircraft division was responsible for the British development of Concorde.

Still within the field of transport, the early twentieth century had seen the rise of new firms drawing on the potential of the internal combustion engine. The mid-twentieth century saw their consolidation into important local industries which ensured that, besides aeroplanes, the name Bristol was to become firmly established with cars and motorbikes, buses and lorries. The first motor car had been built in Bristol in 1900 and its builder, Joseph Barter, went on to develop the Douglas motorcycle, which continued in production in Kingswood until the 1950s. Regular car production in the city had to wait until the formation of the car division of the Bristol Aeroplane Company at the end of the Second World War. Drawing from the in-house expertise in aircraft manufacture and from drawings belonging to the German car maker BMW, confiscated after the war, the company entered the field of luxury car production. The first model, the 400, made its debut in 1947 and established the company's reputation for expensive cars which embodied good detailed design, painstaking hand craftsmanship, speed, power, performance, excellent handling and luxury. Buses had been made in Bristol since 1908 when the Bristol Tramways & Carriage Company started their production at Filton for their own use. In 1912 the BT & CC established new works at Brislington and from the 1920s began the production of bus chassis and lorries for sale nationwide. In the late 1930s the company produced nearly 200 new double-decker buses to replace the trams which finally disappeared in 1941. As part of the Tilling Group, the BT & CC was nationalised in 1948, and the following year the Bristol works introduced the Lodekka, a low-height double-decker which enjoyed widespread use with other nationalised bus companies.

Bristol has a long association with the non-ferrous metal industries, particularly lead working and the making of brass. While brass making finally ended in 1927 with the closure of the works at Keynsham, a new industry – zinc smelting – had started ten years earlier at Avonmouth. The works had been established during the First World War to manufacture poisonous gas but had not been completed before the end of hostilities, and in peacetime they were taken over by the National Smelting Company who commenced zinc smelting and the production of sulphuric acid. Subsequently controlled by the Imperial Smelting Corporation and the Consolidated Zinc Corporation, the undertaking experienced continuous growth throughout the mid-twentieth century, including a programme of modernisation and expansion launched in 1965 in collaboration with Imperial Chemical Industries and Fisons.

The rise of new industries was accompanied by the creation of new industrial zones on the edge of the city. The Bristol Aeroplane Company made Filton an industrial area, while the establishment of the BT & CC's works at Brislington in 1912 was followed by the development of an industrial estate along the Bath Road in the 1920s. An industrial estate was developed in Fishponds and after the war the City Council created a trading estate for light industry in Bedminster. These new industrial zones reflected the diminishing influence of the port in determining the location of new factories. Aeroplane production, for example, existed independently of the port; what was important, however, was the availability of cheap land and the presence of good

Shot Tower, Redcliff Hill, 1940s. The shot tower was built in about 1782 by William Watts, a plumber, who patented a new method of making lead shot in 1782 which apparently came to him in a dream. By Watts' patent, the molten lead was dropped from the top of the tower into a vat of cold water where the droplets solidified into near perfect small balls. Watts' patent completely superseded the old method of casting shot in moulds. The tower survived until 1968, when it was demolished for the widening of Redcliff Hill, but Sheldon Bush and Patent Shot Co., owners of the tower since 1868, continue production in Cheese Lane.

communications by road and rail. The Bristol Aeroplane Company's site at Filton was huge, and after the Second World War even swallowed up the village of Charlton to make way for the new runway required for the Brabazon project.

The development of the industrial estate at Avonmouth was again stimulated by the availability of cheap land and good communications, but also reflected the ability of the port to continue to attract industry. Factory sites adjacent to the quaysides had the advantage that bulky raw materials could be processed with the minimum of movement. As the economic role of the City Docks waned so the attraction of Avonmouth increased, and from the 1920s the Port Authority promoted the Avonmouth Docks Trading Estate at Chittening. Flour milling was gradually concentrated in the docks at Avonmouth, while the metallurgical, chemical and petrochemical industries sustained by imported ores and petroleum were largely responsible for the expansion of the Avonmouth industrial zone northwards along the Severn. The rawness of this industrial development, including the vast works of the National Smelting Company on St Andrew's Road, was emphasised by the survival of small farms such as Rockingham, Chittening and Madam farms immediately outside the factory perimeters.

The city centre, meanwhile, which had traditionally had a strong industrial character owing to the presence of the docks, gradually lost some of its industry during this period. Fry's made the decision to leave the centre in 1922. Their factories were hemmed in on all sides preventing further expansion and there were no direct rail or water communications. They chose a 220-acre site in open country at Keynsham with good communications which they named Somerdale. The move was completed by 1931. Some industries in the centre quietly declined and closed while others, such as Price Powell & Co., stoneware manufacturers in St Thomas Street, were destroyed by German bombing. In the post-war period the granaries and mills in the city closed as the industry consolidated its operations at Avonmouth.

In the post-war period more old-established Bristol industries closed or found their local identity greatly reduced. J.S. Fry & Sons had merged their financial interests with Cadbury's as early as 1918 as a response to intense competition in the industry, and in 1935 became a subsidiary of Cadbury's. Bristol's largest soap manufacturer, Christopher Thomas & Brothers, had been taken over by Lever Brothers in 1913; they were well known locally for the Puritan brand of soap but finally ceased production in 1953. This was not quite the end of Bristol's soap and candle-making industry, however, as Carwardines of Sheene Road, Bedminster, remained in business until about 1961. Locomotive building in Bristol – which had always been on a modest scale compared with Manchester, Leeds or Glasgow – finally came to an end with the closure of Peckett's Atlas works in St George in 1962. The closure of Pountney's Bristol Pottery in Fishponds in 1969 marked the end of a centuries-old Bristol industry. Other industries, meanwhile, thrived: Wills maintained their pre-eminence in cigarette production into the 1960s by relaunching the Embassy brand with gift coupons, which were extremely popular. By the 1960s Robinsons, as part of the Dickinson Robinson Group, had become an international packaging and engineering group. The Bristol Motor Car Company bucked the trend towards absorption, surviving the creation of the British Aircraft Corporation in 1961, when it was bought by Sir George White: production continued, with the Bristol 411 appearing in 1969, although from 1961 they were powered by Chrysler engines made in Canada.

Whatever the shifting fortunes of companies at board level, the prime consideration for thousands of ordinary Bristolians was that local industry meant employment and security. Working conditions varied: some workers endured low pay, long hours and hazardous working conditions. Wills and Fry's, on the other hand, had good reputations in spite of strict and paternalistic regimes on the factory floor. The aim of many young people in Bedminster was to find employment with one of the large firms such as Wills, Robinsons or Mardons. At Wills women would traditionally leave the company upon marrying but there were many employees who spent their entire working lives there. From the 1920s women increasingly found opportunities for office employment, a legacy of the First World War, when they had taken the place of men called to the Front. The larger firms generally had good facilities for their employees: each of the Wills factories had a medical room, treatment room and recreational facilities, including athletic grounds and an evening club in Luckwell Road.

Between 1920 and 1969, several major changes to Bristol's industrial structure occurred. Several industries, including soap and glass manufacture, coal mining and potteries disappeared; ship building ended a few years later with the closure of the Albion yard in the City Docks in 1977 and the clothing and footwear industries diminished in importance. Other industries, however, continued to maintain a strong presence in the city – tobacco, printing and packaging, for example – while new industries such as aircraft production and chemical processing expanded. The rise of manufacturing zones at Avonmouth and Severnside, Filton and Brislington marked the decreasing importance of industry to the city centre. As firms merged, the local identity of the city's manufactures was reduced. By 1969, the influence of the Port on determining the siting of new factories was less important than Bristol's new links by motorway with London, South Wales, the Midlands and the South West. This was a factor in the growth of the service sector, including banking and insurance from the 1960s, a trend which continued through the 1970s and 1980s. As the service sector increased in importance, the number of jobs in manufacturing declined. Traditional skills in engineering and other trades and insustries disappeared and high-rise office blocks – not factories – came to dominate the city centre.

Farriers at work at Fivash, wheelwrights and farriers, St Thomas Street, October 1937. Many traditional handcrafts survived in Bristol into the 1920s and 1930s but declined after the war. In this view a smith operates the bellows while a horshoe is heated in the forge.

Assembling a wheel at Fivash, October 1937. The wheelwright is hammering a felloe (a section of the rim of the wheel) on to the spokes; resting on the nave (the hub) are the remaining two felloes needed to complete the wheel.

Shattock & Hunter, saddlers, Frogmore Street, *c.* 1937. Leather working was traditionally an important trade in the city. Shattock & Hunter were located close to the centre and made saddlery, horse collars, hames and other items of harness.

Byrt Brothers, Netham Cooperage, Redfield, Bristol, *c.* 1937. A beautifully lit photograph inside the Netham cooperage showing a cooper pulling the staves of a barrel together. There was a large demand for barrels in Bristol and in the mid-1930s there were sixteen coopers at work in the city; by 1968–9 only Byrt Brothers survived, and they had gone by 1970.

Basketing jars at Price Powell & Co., Thomas Street Pottery, *c.* 1937. The company formerly had as many as thirty basket-makers at work making basket-ware covers to protect the large wine and spirit jars made for the Christmas trade. Price's made a wide range of functional stoneware products including bottles and jars for cider, soft drinks and ink.

Gervase Thorne throwing a two-gallon stoneware bottle at Price's, *c.* 1937. A foreman potter, Thorne had worked for the company for fifty years. Stoneware manufacture had flourished in the city since the early eighteenth century; Price's business dated to 1796 but came to an abrupt end when their works were bombed in November 1940.

he workshop of Douglas Cleverdon, printer and publisher, Great George Street, *c.* 1937. The photograph shows Frank
ucker (1911–1946) operating an Albion hand press made by Hopkinson & Cope, Finsbury, London.

William Terrell & Sons' rope works at Brislington, 1938. Terrell's were established at Welsh Back in the 1820s, moving to Canon's Marsh in the 1880s and to a new works at Brislington in 1902. They made all sizes of rope up to 4-in hawsers and also held the contract for braided piston packing for locomotives of the Great Western Railway. They were taken over by British Ropes in 1964 and closed the following year.

Hutchings & Skewes Brothers, tailors, 85 Park Street, c. 1937. The photograph shows the tailor sitting cross-legged ironing the lapel of a jacket. In the foreground is a sleeve board and in the background numerous tailors' dummies.

Henry Simmons Ltd, hatters, 12 St James Barton, c. 1937. Bristol was well known for hat making in the nineteenth century although the industry was in decline by the 1920s. In 1940 Simmons were advertising themselves as manufacturers of uniform hats and caps, hand-made bowlers and silk top hats. George Ewens, who is seen here, worked for Simmons and was the last top hat maker in Bristol. He is seen applying the plush silk covering to the calico foundation by means of a hot iron.

The Board of Directors of J.S. Fry & Sons pose for the camera in the board room of the company's Union Street premises in 1928, the bicentenary year, sitting under a portrait of Joseph Storrs Fry (1826–1913). C.R. Fry, sixth in descent from Joseph Fry (1728–87), founder of the firm, is second from the right and E. Cadbury is on the right.

Nut roasting at Fry's, Somerdale, Keynsham, 1932. Roasting the cocoa beans was the first process in the making of either cocoa or chocolate. It was a delicate process requiring skill and careful judgement, as the quality and aromatic flavour of the finished product depended upon the success of this operation. The roasters at Somerdale consisted of huge revolving ovens, which could hold about half a ton of beans and were heated by gas.

Fry's Easter egg and novelty catalogue for Easter 1934. On the cover chicks march out of the new factory site at Somerdale, Keynsham, developed in the 1920s. Until the early 1970s Fry's produced catalogues every year advertising a wide range of fancy chocolates for Easter and Christmas, to supplement their staple range of Five Boys, Turkish Delight, Crunchie, Fry's Cream Bars and drinking cocoas.

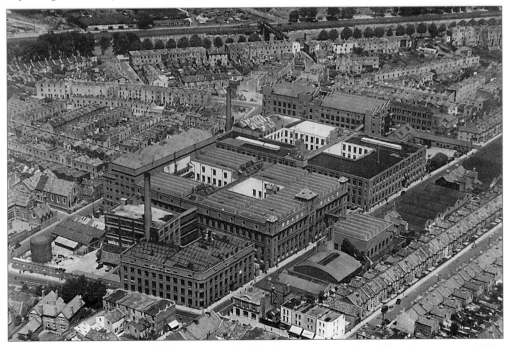

Aerial view of W.D. & H.O. Wills' factories in Raleigh Road towering over the neighbouring streets, *c.* 1950.

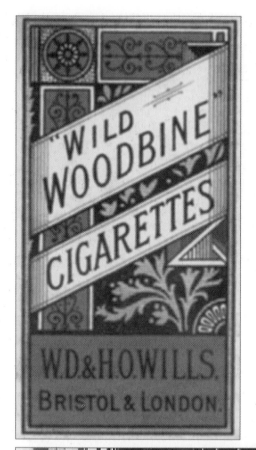

Many famous brands of tobacco, cigarettes and cigars have been produced by Wills: Golden Virginia has long maintained the position as the leading handrolling tobacco. The first cigarette brand was Bristol, introduced in 1871. Three Castles appeared in 1878 and Woodbine, which for years was Britain's most popular cigarette, was introduced in 1888. Cigarette cards, printed by Mardons, were originally introduced as packet stiffeners in 1878 and remained popular until 1939. Embassy was introduced in 1914 and was successfully relaunched in 1962 as a coupon cigarette. The coupons were very popular, and within three years had helped Wills achieve nearly 40 per cent of the UK cigarette market by weight and 34 per cent by count: one in four cigarettes sold was an Embassy brand.

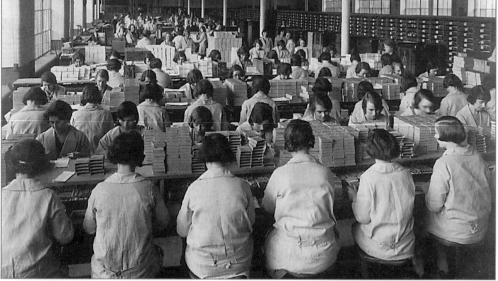

Packing cigarettes by hand, W.D. & H.O. Wills, *c.* 1936. By the twentieth century the cigarette was established as the most popular form of tobacco and, using cigarette machines, were produced by the million; the trays of finished cigarettes were conveyed to the packing department where they were packed at speed, although here large cartons are being filled by hand.

John Harvey inspecting by candlelight a commemorative magnum of Bristol Cream sherry produced for the 1953 coronation; the bottles, which are being filled from a hand bottling machine, were held against the candlelight to ensure that the wine was clear. This was Harvey's first commemorative bottling, and the bottles were given a special label bearing the Queen's monogram.

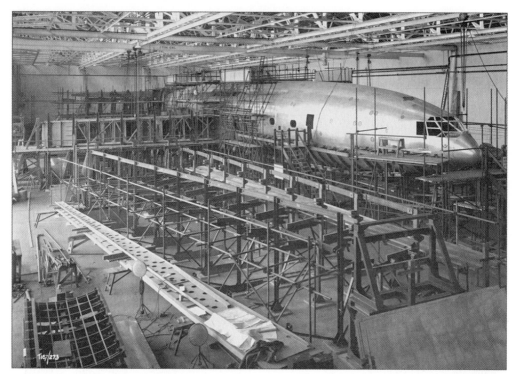

The Bristol Brabazon (G-AGPW) under construction in its specially built hanger at Filton in about 1947. This aircraft was named after Lord Brabazon, chairman of a committee set up in 1942 to consider Britain's post-war aviation needs, and was developed as a trans-oceanic airliner capable of flying non-stop between London and New York. When it made its maiden flight on 4 September 1949 it was the world's largest civil aeroplane, but in 1952 the project was cancelled – and this prototype was scrapped the following year.

Bristol 170 Freighter, *c.* 1950. This aircraft originated as a military freighter towards the end of the war, and the prototype flew on 2 December 1945. It was developed through several variants, most of which had the large nose doors for ease of freight loading, although the 'Wayfarer' seen here was an all-passenger version built without this feature. Altogether 214 Bristol Freighters were built, and for some twenty-five years this noisy, ungainly but useful aircraft was a familiar sight in British airspace.

Bristol type 401 saloon at the Clifton Suspension Bridge, *c.* 1950. This carefully posed shot of the latest product of the car division of the Bristol Aeroplane Group under the massive chain links of Brunel's suspension bridge shows two contrasting Bristol engineering achievements that were a century apart. The 401 was introduced in the autumn of 1949 as a four-seater two-door saloon; drawing on the company's expertise in aircraft design it was one of the most aerodynamically efficient cars of its time. Production continued until 1953, by which time 650 had been made.

Engine fitter at work on a bus chassis, Bristol Commercial Vehicles, Brislington, 1937. A particular feature of bus production was that the manufacture of the chassis and the bodywork were undertaken separately. Bristol-made bus chassis carried bodies made by several different companies including Eastern Coach Works. The works closed in 1983.

Smith's Potato Crisps factory, Bath Road, Brislington, *c.* 1935. This trading estate was developed from the 1920s with some stylish factories facing the A4.

Puritan soap packet by Christopher Thomas & Brothers, Broad Plain, *c.* 1950. The company was founded in 1825 and Puritan bar soap introduced in 1898. In the 1920s and 1930s gift coupons were issued with Puritan soap, and from 1936 until the scheme was withdrawn in 1939, the company had a gift shop in St Augustine's Parade.

CHAPTER TWELVE

THE CITY CENTRE

B etween 1920 and 1969 Bristol's city centre experienced a radical transformation – radical enough, as the photographic record illustrates, to render large parts of the centre of the 1920s and 1930s unrecognisable by the 1960s. The pre-war city centre had changed little since the late nineteenth century when St Augustine's Bridge at the head of the Frome was built, the Tramway Centre established and several important street schemes, such as the extension of Baldwin Street, completed. Then came the war. The blitz caused the destruction of many familiar and much-loved landmarks like the timber-framed Dutch House; several churches were badly damaged and the main shopping centre along Wine Street and Castle Street largely reduced to a desolate bomb site. The subsequent comprehensive replanning – notably the relocation of the shopping centre at Broadmead – marked a break with the past, but some important changes to the city centre had started before the war, particularly in response to a perceived need to provide the city with a new, larger council building in a more dignified setting – and also to deal with the greatest problem of all: traffic.

The role of the City's planners, engineers and some architects in grappling with the problems of adapting an old city centre to the requirements of the twentieth century exposed the deep differences that can exist between professional and popular opinion. The planners came to regard the densely packed pre-war centre as a monument to the 'mistakes of the past'. The city, they saw, lacked a focus – the jumble of Georgian and Victorian buildings lining the Frome unworthy of a large and important city. They saw Bristol's city centre as a place of appalling chaos: overcrowded housing, shops, offices, churches and factories compressed along narrow roads congested with traffic; and a centre that also lacked open space.

The congestion could not be doubted: in 1934 J.B. Priestley described the centre of Bristol with some affection as 'a place where trams and coastal steamers seemed in danger of a collision'. The centre clearly lacked a formal and symbolic central focus but instead had several that were genuine and practical: the Tramway Centre – a raised triangle of pavement above St Augustine's Bridge where trams (until 1939), buses and taxis provided the physical means of connection between the centre and the suburbs;

Corn Street – which served as the business and commercial heart of the city; and Wine Street and Castle Street further east – which formed the main shopping centre and also a social focus, a place where people promenaded on Saturday and Sunday evenings. The scale was human and intimate, with narrow streets crammed with a wealth of architectural variety – from medieval timber framing to Edwardian baroque in brick and Bath stone. But as J.B. Priestley observed, Bristol had not gone quaint: it was also a busy modern commercial centre, and factory chimneys vied with church spires for prominence on the skyline. And the city was not without its open space: Queen's Square, College Green and several churchyards offered quiet seclusion without detracting from the overall cohesion of the cityscape; but these were not the wide-open formal spaces which the planners desired.

The inadequacy of the old Council House had been apparent since the early 1900s, and in 1919 the City set up a special committee to consider a scheme for acquiring a site for municipal buildings on College Green. Progress was slow, and it was not until 1933 that E. Vincent Harris was appointed architect of the scheme. The designs were approved the following year, and in 1935 old property on College Green was demolished to make way for the site and the foundation stone was laid. By the outbreak of war the building was largely completed. Harris had designed a long, curved neo-Georgian building facing the city centre. It is a sombre, dignified building, but has attracted criticism for the preponderance of the hipped roof and for its unusual domed central porch. The Council decided to use pale brown hand-made bricks from Moreton-in-Marsh, Gloucestershire, as the principal facing material so that the importance of the cathedral should not be challenged. This sensitivity to the immediate surroundings contrasts with the decision taken after the war to lower the level of College Green in response to the architect's request that it would 'make' his building; unfortunately the felling of the mature trees together with the removal of the railings and the replica high cross has been widely condemned, creating in the words of Professor J.V. Punter 'a billiard table wasteland of flat lawns and aimless paths'.

The problem of traffic congestion was not new. In the second half of the nineteenth century several important changes were made to routes through the centre to ease the flow of traffic. What was new after 1920 was the rise in private ownership of the motor car: between the end of the First World War and 1930 the number of cars in Britain increased from about 200,000 to over one million. Congestion worsened and motorists began complaining about the shortage of places to park. Bristol was the meeting place of eleven main roads, including two national routes which intersected at St Augustine's Parade: the A4 linking Avonmouth with London and the A38 from the Midlands to the south-west. In 1936 the City began work on the creation of an inner circuit road intended to link the major routes and thus lessen the volume of traffic in the centre. A new thoroughfare, Temple Way, cut a new course to the south from Old Market towards Temple Meads, crossing the Floating Harbour by a new bridge at Temple Back. The route continued westwards into Redcliffe Way. Here the road ran close to the north porch of St Mary Redcliffe and caused the demolition of the corner of Pile Street and St Thomas Street. After crossing the docks by a new bridge the road then cut diagonally across Queen Square, effectively destroying the peace and tranquillity of this eighteenth-century square and leaving Rysbrack's equestrian statue of William III stranded on a central traffic island. Beyond the square, where the road met Prince Street and King Street, a roundabout was built which involved the demolition of the Merchants Arms public house. In the centre the flow of traffic between Redcliffe Way and College Green was simplified by covering in a stretch of the Frome below St Augustine's Bridge. This modification transformed the centre: Broad Quay lost its waterfront and the shops on St Augustines Parade no longer looked over to ships. Effectively, Bristol's 'street of ships' had disappeared – and all of this was completed before the first bomb fell on Bristol.

The Blitz during the evening of 24 November 1940 caused widespread devastation to Bristol. In the centre it wiped out much of Wine Street and Castle Street. Mary-le-Port Street, a quaint, narrow thoroughfare, was destroyed; so too was the Dutch House – a much photographed timber-framed house on the corner of Wine Street and the High Street – and, saddest of all, St Peter's Hospital, a fifteenth-century merchant's house (see *Bristol 1850–1919*, page 112). There were more losses over the ensuing months. Many Bristolians, it is clear, felt disorientation and a deep sense of loss at the destruction of familiar surroundings, but the planners saw things differently. The clearing of the site by enemy bombs, in their view, enormously simplified the problem and provided a unique opportunity to replan the centre.

In 1942 a Planning and Reconstruction Committee was created by the City, and two years later released plans for a radical reshaping of the city. The *Evening Post* described them as 'bold beyond the wildest dreams of most people'. Traffic remained a prime consideration (the City Engineer recommended the addition of an inner ring road to intercept the major radial roads), but the most radical idea was the creation of separate zones for civic use, shopping and education in place of the former mixture and diversity of land use in the centre. Thus a large tract of land was set aside on St Michael's Hill and Kingsdown for the expansion of the university on the western side and the hospitals to the east. The Wine Street/Castle Street area was to become a new cultural centre with a concert hall, museum and art gallery, while the shopping centre was to be relocated to a new site at Broadmead. Industry would be moved to new sites in the suburbs where factories, housing, schools and recreational facilities would be grouped in 'neighbourhood units'.

The relocation of the shopping centre to Broadmead was the suggestion that caused greatest concern. Wine Street and Castle Street formed a popular and valuable shopping centre linking east and west Bristol, and it was felt by many that removing the shops would result in the sterilisation of a large and important area in the heart of the city. The traders were anxious to resume business there as soon as possible: Broadmead was off the beaten track in their view, and the support of the multiple traders for Broadmead (their major competitors) only strengthened their opposition. A poll of shoppers organised by the Bristol Retail Trades Federation in 1947 demonstrated overwhelming support for the old shopping centre: 13,363 votes in favour as opposed to 418 votes for Broadmead. The government response was also lukewarm. The City's grand vision, they considered, was inappropriate in a climate of austerity, and in 1947 the Government cut Bristol's redevelopment plans.

The City, however, was adamant that Broadmead was the better option – offering a less restricted site where shops would benefit from wider frontages. So they pressed ahead, albeit with a much reduced plan. The decision to demolish the Lower Arcade was reversed in response to protests from the Council for the Protection of Ancient Bristol and others. But the more fundamental objections to the Broadmead scheme voiced by local traders and architects were largely ignored. In 1952 Sir John Inskip, Chairman of the Planning and Reconstruction Committee, confidently asserted: 'I picture Broadmead during the next few years a hive of building activity and within the coming decade a vista of pleasant shops and do I hear some of our present-day critics saying, "they were right"?' The arrogance of local politicians, their failure to involve interested parties in the decision-making process and the compulsory land purchases enforced in Broadmead created a deep feeling of antipathy from a wide section of the Bristol public towards the City Council – and their new shopping centre.

Broadmead, a council shopping estate, exhibited the same dull uniformity that characterised its housing estates. The retention of the Greyhound Hotel, Quakers' Friars and the Lower Arcade provided some degree of visual relief but generally the new shopping centre lacked the variety and character of the old. The City Architect wished for 'good, simple and dignified architecture', but most of the new shops were bland in the extreme. And, paradoxically, while the City treated the smaller traders in an arbitrary and high-handed manner it readily capitulated to the demands of the more powerful multiple companies, many of whom used their own in-house architects to design their stores and, like Woolworths, insisted on their standard fascias. By 1954 the first phase of Broadmead and Union Street was complete. The next phase saw new shops introduced as far as Penn Street by 1956, resulting in the demolition of old property in Merchant Street and the total eradication of Old King Street, Rosemary Street and Milk Street from the city centre map. Many old buildings, including several public houses, disappeared. The third phase, which took the number of shops in Broadmead to a total of 148, extended as far as Broad Weir and the Inner Circuit Road and was completed by 1960. Dull and characterless, deserted after 6.00 pm in the evenings, Broadmead failed to provide the new focus that the planners had hoped for. The old shopping centre, meanwhile, remained a desolate wasteland – a vacuum in the heart of the city – as plans for the new civic and cultural centre were postponed as the Council turned to the more pressing need to provide new housing.

Beyond Broadmead, other developments were to pull apart the old centre and its immediate surroundings and destroy its coherence. In response to the 1947 Town & Country Planning Act, which required local authorities to produce plans and take control of new development, the City Council published its first Development Plan in 1952. For the central area this involved the completion of the Inner Circuit Road from Old Market to St James's Barton and thence via Bond Street and Lewins Mead to Colston Avenue. Completion of this in the 1950s and 1960s cut a swathe through old Bristol north and west of the Broadmead shopping centre: streets were realigned and widened, and shops and many historic buildings disappeared as considerations of traffic flow outweighed any sentiment for the past. The plan also sanctioned the development of university and hospital extensions in Kingsdown, and here from the mid-1950s large parts of this picturesque Georgian suburb were destroyed to make way for new university and hospital buildings. Similarly, the development of a new entertainment complex in Frogmore Street in the mid-1960s resulted in the large-scale demolition of a maze of picturesque old streets and lanes overlooking the centre. Within the centre itself much of the City's radical vision disintegrated under waves of office developments, over which the Council exerted, at best, weak and vacillating control.

From about 1959 until the early 1970s the centre fell victim to a boom in office building, which coincided with a vogue for high-rise towers and blocks. Within the space of a few years the historic city skyline – a harmonious mix of church towers, spires and cupolas, rooftops and chimneys of many varieties which had taken centuries to evolve – was ruined. Bristol's first post-war office building, Gaunt's House, overlooking College Green, was completed in 1952; this steel-framed block faced in Bath stone anticipated subsequent office developments, not only in the method of construction but also the way in which the sheer bulk of the building dwarfed its immediate surroundings, including the Lord Mayor's chapel; it also paid scant regard to the medieval street plan. In 1961 the Council released land on the corner of the High Street and Wine Street earmarked for civic use – to an insurance company and the Bank of England. Despite strong public opposition the construction of the Norwich Union building and the Bank of England went ahead, but the two buildings failed miserably to do justice to this prominent site in the heart of the old medieval city.

Much of the office building in the mid-1960s was speculative, fuelled by the 22 per cent increase in growth of the service sector in Bristol between 1961 and 1969. Nevertheless, the first office block to have a major impact on the city centre skyline belonged to a company with strong local roots: this was the fifteen-storey Robinson building built on the site of their Victorian premises near Bristol Bridge in 1965. At the time of its construction this tower block, over 200 ft tall, was considerably higher than anything else in the city centre, and while the façades exhibited careful detailed design the building still jarred with its immediate surroundings through its sheer size and the choice of white pre-cast concrete as the facing material. In the absence of a high buildings policy from the Council – who themselves were building high-rise blocks of flats across the city at this time – other tall blocks in the centre soon followed: Tower House in Fairfax Street, the South West Regional Government offices in the Pithay, occupying a commanding site on the centre, the Bristol & West building, and St Lawrence House, twelve storeys high, which towered over the neighbouring spire of St John's-in-the-Wall. The intrusion of these drab, dreary blocks of concrete and glass within a relatively short period took place to mounting criticism, especially as some of them replaced fine Victorian and Edwardian commercial buildings.

In 1966 the City Council published a Development Plan Review. It was dominated by a spirit of uncompromising modernism: there was no high buildings policy, despite mounting pressure for one. Highway schemes still dominated the planners' thinking, and it was these which caused the greatest opposition. Traffic congestion continued to grow as car ownership in Bristol continued to rise: in 1948 there were 20,000 private car owners in the city, and between 1950 and 1961 car ownership doubled. The free circulation of traffic was seen as the greatest priority and the Review proposed a vertical segregation of road traffic and pedestrians in the centre by creating pedestrian decks above the roads, while an outer circuit road would intercept incoming traffic. The plans required the comprehensive redevelopment of large tracts of central Bristol, while the road system would have resulted in laying waste large parts of the inner suburbs. Work on the outer circuit road began, cutting a swathe through Easton and resulting in the demolition of 550 houses in Totterdown, but that was as far as the new road system got. By 1973 the plan was rendered obsolete by a fundamental shift in national policy on urban road schemes – a response to growing concern for the environmental consequences of urban roads. The same year saw the collapse of the commercial property market and the end of the era of slab and tower office building. When the property market recovered in the late 1970s the climate of opinion had undergone a fundamental shift: planners came to see the merits of conservation and public consultation, and taking public opinion into account became an integral part of the planning process. Modernism was out of fashion and the primacy of motor traffic was no longer taken for granted, but together the Blitz and mid-twentieth-century planning philosophies have left their indelible mark on Bristol's city centre.

The view down Broad Street to St John's Gateway from the Grand Hotel, early 1930s: a picturesque roof top view of the city centre on a sunny morning before the scene was altered by post-war developments. There is a strong flavour of Gothic architecture to the scene, with the roof of the Guildhall in the centre. Designed by the Bristol architect, Richard Shackleton Pope, in the Perpendicular style, the Guildhall was built in 1843 to provide more suitable accommodation for the courts, but from the first was criticised because of its inadequacy and inconvenience. Broad Street ends at St John's Gateway, the only medieval gateway in the city wall to survive, which supports the fourteenth-century tower and spire of St John's church. To the right of the spire, in the distance, St Michael's church in Kingsdown can be seen. The photograph was taken before Electricity House was built on a site bounded by Rupert Street, Nelson Street and Christmas Street; designed by Sir Giles Scott, the building was begun in 1936 and completed after the war.

Three familiar Bristol landmarks punctuate the skyline: on the left is Cabot Tower, built to commemorate the 400th anniversary of the discovery of Newfoundland by John Cabot who sailed from Bristol; to the right is the tower of the Wills university building, designed by Sir George Oatley; and further right again is the square gothic block of the Physics Building of 1929, which was also the work of Oatley. Also dating to 1929 but of a very different character is the bright, modernistic Northcliffe House, centre left, premises of the *Evening World* in Colston Avenue. After the war the Kingsdown hillside overlooking the centre was unsympathetically developed with hospital and university extensions, while St John's church was dwarfed by St Lawrence House, a large office block built in 1967.

St John's Gateway, 1920s. The view of Broad Street looking through St John's Gateway has been a popular subject with photographers ever since the early days of photography in the 1850s. The Grand Hotel built in 1868 is on the left in front of Christ Church. The timber-framed Dutch House can just be glimpsed on the corner of Wine Street and the High Street.

Martins Bank, on the corner of Corn Street and Small Street, late 1930s. This handsome classical building in the commercial heart of Bristol was designed by James Weir, a London architect, and was built by the London and South Western Bank on the site of St Werburgh's church. The church was demolished in 1878 and the banking house opened in 1880; it is now a Wetherspoon's pub.

Corn Street, 1930s: a pre-war view of the east end of Corn Street, with the Dutch House visible on the corner of the High Street. The tower of All Saints' church was added by William Paul and George Townsend between 1712 and 1717 and the cupola by Luke Henwood in 1807. On the right is the imposing Palladian façade of the Exchange built in 1741–3 to the design of John Wood; the Coffee House alongside was designed by Thomas Paty in 1782.

The Dutch House, corner of Wine Street and High Street, *c.* 1930. This merchant's house of 1676 was a well-known city centre landmark, and in the 1920s and 1930s was occupied by the Irish Linen and Hosiery Association. It was damaged beyond repair in the air raid of 24 November 1940, and in 1964 the Bank of England building was built on the site.

Host Street, 1930s. A dramatic, night-time view of sixteenth-century timber-framed houses in Host Street illuminated, it would seem, by floodlights. They contained a well-known fried fish shop and a medieval arch, a fragment of St Bartholomew's Hospital, founded before 1207.

No. 33 King Street from the corner of King William Street, *c.* 1930. King Street, immediately south of the city walls, was laid out in about 1650–60 and named by a loyal Corporation in celebration of the Restoration of King Charles II in 1660. This timber-framed gabled house of the late seventeenth century is crammed in between nineteenth-century warehouses, and contains a section of the old city wall in its structure.

The corner of Union Street and Nelson Street, 1936. Fry's imposing granite and brick corner office block was demolished early in 1937 and replaced by the Odeon Cinema, which opened in June 1938.

The author suggests that this slip be inserted in a suitable position in the second volume.

"BRISTOL AS IT WAS 1914-1900" Amendments

Page 14 : All horse tram services electrified by December, 1900.

Plate 4 : This bus route was via Clare St., Wine St., Castle St., Carey's Lane, Stratton St., and Sussex Place.

Plate 19 : The term " Growler " was only used in London. In Bristol and the provinces the vehicle was known as a " Fly ", or four-wheeled cab.

Plate 23 : The sign showing a bell indicated a telephone ; no connection with Edison Bell. The motor vehicle seen was a " Red Taxi " (of the Provincial Taxi Co.). First licenced at the same time as the " Blue Taxis " : July 1908.

Plate 24 : Until the roadway was lowered under the railway bridge near Eastville Park it was necessary to use the smaller trams on the Fishponds Road.
These small trams had three windows and 15 of them were delivered by the American Car Co. in 1895, Bristol's first electric trams. (Numbered 86-97, 116-118.)

Plate 30 : The s.s. *Demerara* was launched and wrecked in 1851, but the " s.s." was only a courtesy title because she was on her way to have her engines installed at the time of her loss. The accident happened near the lower Zig-Zag (not Horseshoe Bend). The figurehead fell to pieces from neglect for the want of a canopy.

Plate 36 : Between the Art Gallery and the Blind Asylum Chapel is seen an archway which led to the H.Q. of the Rifle Volunteers (later 4th Gloucesters).

Plate 41 : Four readers have kindly offered explanations of the word " Entire " :—
It was beer brewed from charred malt (also sold by Masters in Broadmead, Plate 76).
It was an abbreviation of " Entire Butt Beer ", an old name for Porter, or what we now call Stout.
It meant the opposite of Free House, meaning that the entire ownership of that public house belonged to D. Sykes & Co.
It was another name for a stallion ; in those days all horse dealers had to know where such an animal was kept.

Plate 42 : The ship is the *Clio* : built 1873, bought by the Admiralty in 1914, and sunk as a block ship at Scapa Flow.

Plate 45 : This view shows the organ as from 19 Sept. 1903 in the new Colston Hall that was opened in 1901 ; it was enlarged a few years later so that the pipes filled the alcoves left and right. In 1936 the organ was rebuilt and enlarged and given an elaborate gilt fronted grille. It was this that was destroyed in the 1945 fire.

Plate 49 : Remains of old houses demolished and new building erected 1958.

Plate 52 : 1903 Humberette 5 h.p. ($6\frac{1}{2}$ and $7\frac{1}{2}$ h.p. models also available in 1905). Single spoke steering wheel ; driver's large lever was a brake lever operating band brakes on rear wheels, (seen behind hubs, through the spokes) ; a water cooled engine (most small runabouts then were air cooled). Another authority suggests that it was a 1903 Humber single cylinder Voiturette.

Plate 57 : 1902 unlikely as mid-day services not then held.

Plate 58 : Suggested that postman's hat was called a " gravyboat ".

Plate 69 : Meat Market demolished 1913.

Plate 79 : *Robert* Aldworth.

Plate 82 : Carved overmantel (not fireplace) believed to be by Grinling Gibbons.

Plate 88 : Owned by Mr. J. R. Watson, O.B.E., Chief Constable of Bristol, who is seen at the wheel. Taken about 1923. The make is a 1918 Buick ; or a Cadillac-type 57 roadster, in production from 1918/20, or an Overland about 1920. Delete reference to Stepney spare wheel—it was the standard wood artillery wheel with demountable rim common to most American and many European cars until nearly 1930.

Plate 91 : 1908 was the date of the first two country bus services.

Plate 93 : Vehicle shown was first licenced 19 Nov., 1907. The Westbury to Redland route started early in 1908.

Plate 94 : On the model seen, the locking wheel for the brake was actuated by the foot. The large wheel, familiar on later trams, was used to set the shoe brake.

Plate 96 : Semaphore lighting is visible just below the gong : yellow for Horfield, green for Durdham Down ; blue for Fishponds ; white for Staple Hill. (Red could not be used on the front, only the rear).

Plate 106 : A composite fireplace consisting of fragments taken from several others, not necessarily Jacobean.

Plate 111 : " Victoria & Albert ", not " Britannia " !

Plate 113 : No explanation of " Fum-Fum " has been received.

Plate 128 : The pigs were en route from Ireland via Hotwells to Pig Factors in West St., Old Market. Arriving very lean, the animals were fattened up for 4-5 weeks.

Plate 130 : This group of houses was on an island site in the middle of Broad Weir at the approaches to Ellbroad St. and Narrow Weir (approx. the site of the grass plot by the Penn St./Broad Weir junction).

Plate 133 : Not " MIORAMA ", (Possibly Panorama, or Diorama). Contemporary newspapers give " Poole's MYRIORAMA ".

Plate 134 : " near the site of Prince St. roundabout ".

Plate 139 : This is one of John Payne's tugs, most of which were built at his Vauxhall yard on the Cut.

Plates 146 and 148 : Not the Cran Brook. It was Cutler's Mill Brook that ran down the back of Elton Rd. to the junction of Cheltenham and Zetland Roads (and behind the Colston Girls' School to Rennison's Bath ; there to join the Froom through low-lying land at Sussex Place.)

Plates 148 and 150 : Taken by a schoolboy who sold over 3,000 copies at 2d. each, in two weeks home from school.

Plate 151 : The figure at the foot of the post may be a points boy. The shelter was a waiting room for passengers, provided by the B.T.C.C.

Plate 153 : Trams ran to Staple Hill in 1905.

Plate 155 : Road widening caused the removal of the trees on the left ; complaints of dampness, those on the right.

Plate 167 : The vehicle is a White steam car, 10 h.p., 1903-4, £380 or £400. The steering wheel knob could be a quadrant control.

Plate 169 : For white ring on " black ", read " red ". (Red photographed as black, before the days of red sensitive emulsions).

Plate 170 : The boy in the second row, kneeling, first from left, is Douglas Cleverdon, the well-known B.B.C. producer.

Plate 172 : Carried 22 passengers.

Page 79 : Horse drawn tram, not bus. AE 725 registered 27 August 1907.

Kindly contributed by " A Monthly Bulletin " ; the Rev. E. C. Pritchard ; the late Charles Thomas ; Messrs. P. M. Alexander, M. Beale, G. P. Biggs, R. C. Brooks, H. Cottrell, H. A. Cracknell, H. H. Davis, G. Farr, D. C. Gass, G. M. Green, D. Hodgson, L. A. Humphreys, F. C. Jones, E. R. Keen, J. Machin, B. Ord, C. Phillips, A. J. Phippen, H. E. Reed, C. G. Rich, K. H. Rosewell, D. G. Rowland, E. N. Short, H. W. Stevens, M. J. Tozer, L. E. Trott, S. Vowles, J. Warburton, C. J. Warren ; and as a result of the author's further researches.

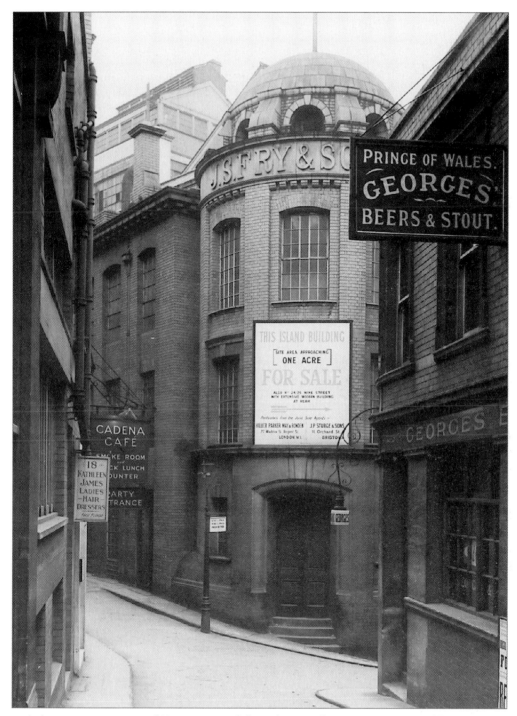

Fry's factory no. 7, corner of Tower Lane and the Pithay, 6 February 1938. Designed by Sir George Oatley and built in 1905, this factory was made redundant when Fry's moved to Keynsham. After serving as Her Majesty's Stationery Office, it was demolished in 1964 to make way for Pithay House, an office block belonging to Capital & Counties. The Cadena café was one of several in the city from about 1909, and the Prince of Wales was one of the many George's pubs in the city.

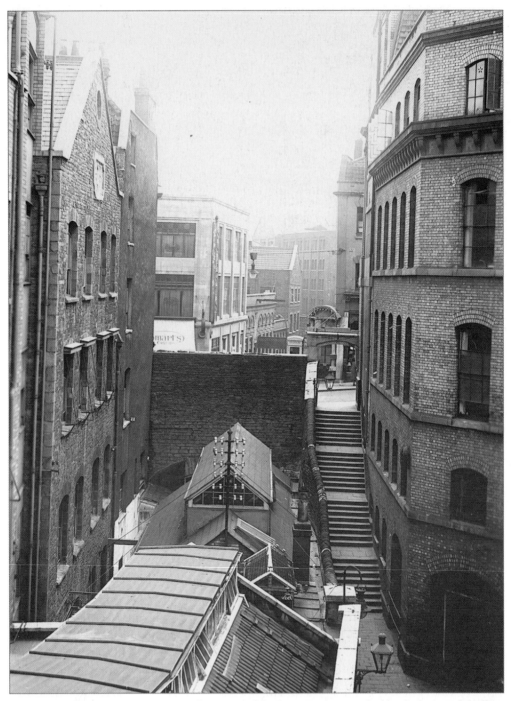

The Frome under Union Street, 1936. The course of the River Frome is marked by the low-roofed offices belonging to J.S. Fry's, in a yard which is occupied by the present-day route of Fairfax Street. Fry's factories loom over the space on the left, while the large brick building on the right of the steps leading up to Union Street belonged to Ferris & Co., wholesale druggists, established 1754. Smart Brothers' furnishing store is across the road on the corner of Union Street and Fairfax Street, which follows the line of the river into the distance.

Union Street, 1936. This was photographed shortly before the Fry's showrooms and offices on the left were demolished and replaced by the Odeon cinema and new shops.

The newly completed Union Street Bridge, *c*. 1953.

Union Street, 21 August 1938. Fry's new showrooms maintain the presence of the firm in Union Street, which dated from 1777. On the corner is the new Odeon cinema, designed by T. Cecil Howitt, which had opened the previous month.

Upper Arcade, *c*. 1950. Designed by James Foster and built in 1824, the Upper Arcade ran between St James's Barton and the Horsefair. It was destroyed by bombing in 1940, and in this view, taken before the ruins were cleared for new shops in Broadmead, the Ionic columns of the entrance frame 12 St James's Barton, an impressive house of 1728 that was demolished in 1960.

City centre bomb site, *c*. 1950. Cellars of buildings destroyed in the Blitz below the ruins of St Peter's church provide extra parking in the heart of the pre-war shopping centre. In 1944 this area was zoned for civic use by the City Council's Planning and Reconstruction Committee, but the plans were first delayed and then abandoned.

Milk Street, *c*. 1950. Two public houses are seen here – the Lamb & Anchor and the Crown & Cushion. Both dated to at least the late eighteenth century, being listed in Mathew's Bristol Directory for 1794, but they were demolished along with the rest of the street in the mid-1950s to make way for the building of the second phase of the Broadmead shopping centre.

Rosemary Street, *c*. 1950. These Georgian houses were demolished in about 1954 and the street disappeared under an eastern extension of Broadmead beyond Merchant Street.

Offices and works of E.S. & A. Robinson Ltd, cardboard box and paper bag manufacturers, near Bristol Bridge in Victoria Street shortly before demolition in 1961. This imposing brick building was designed by William Bruce Gingell and built in 1876. The building had a chequered history, being partially destroyed by fire in 1903 and then badly damaged in the war when the corner tower lost its large dome. Notwithstanding its forlorn appearance, the building preserves the exuberance of Gingell's original design, with a variety of arch patterns and mouldings in brick. The Robinson Group built a fifteen-storey block in its place, which at over 200 ft in height became a dominant city centre landmark.

King Street, c. 1961. St Nicholas Almshouses on the corner with Queen Charlotte Street date from 1652. In this view the almshouses are in a poor state of repair; they were renovated during the 1960s but lost something of their character in the process: the tall chimney-stacks and the moulded drip courses above the ground floor windows were removed. The low gabled roof of the almshouses is dwarfed by the Palladian façade of the Cooper's Hall, designed by William Halfpenny. Next again is the Theatre Royal, the oldest playhouse in the country, which opened in 1766.

Rupert Street looking towards the Horsefair, *c.* 1950. The extension of the Inner Circuit Road through Lewins Mead and 1960s office developments resulted in the removal of much old property, including the Bristol United Breweries (taken over by its local rival George's in 1956) on the left. The brewery was an attractive building with a façade of yellow brick with red string courses. The Fire Brigade station, opened in 1930, is on the right.

The Cathedral and College Green, *c.* 1930: an old-established green bounded by the Cathedral and the Lord Mayor's chapel. In this view the statue of Queen Victoria by Sir J.E. Boehm, erected in 1888 to commemorate her Golden Jubilee in 1887, is seen against a backdrop of trees which were felled between 1950 and 1951 – when College Green was re-landscaped upon the completion of the Council House.

e Tramway Centre from College Green, September 1937. The towers of St Stephen's church, Christ Church, All nts' and shops on Broad Quay reflect the early evening sunshine under a brooding, overcast sky. This view had changed le since St Augustine's Bridge had been built at the head of the culverted Frome in 1893, but work on covering the en section of water seen here had already begun and the Dublin Shed, the port's first transit shed, had been demolished e year before; at the time of this photograph its site was serving as a temporary car park (below the Bovril sign). By the nmer of the following year the culvert for the river was well advanced and was completed in 1940. The landscaping of e large central island, however, was delayed until after the war.

Three trams can be seen below the trees in Colston Avenue and these will leave the centre for ever in two years' time; e of the double-decker buses which were to replace the trams in large numbers is approaching the camera. Horse-awn traffic, however, remains in evidence and a covered wagon is seen leaving Canon's Road. Neon advertising signs are rticularly prominent on the shops on Broad Quay: the dominance of the giant Bovril sign is testimony to the power of vertising. These signs were a victim of air-raid precautions which involved a nightly 'black-out', and did not reappear er the war. A more conventional sign board on the extreme right of the view advertises Coast Lines Seaway's services all parts of Britain. The telephone box is an early K1 model of pre-cast concrete, first introduced in 1923.

Radiant House, Colston Street, the headquarters of the Bristol Gas Company, was partially rebuilt in the modern-style architecture which began to appear in the city centre after 1930. The new façade with its curved windows – typical of the 1930s – was designed by Whinney Son and Austen Hall and opened on 29 March 1935. The side façade is part of the original 1904 building, designed by William Venn Gough. The building was lit not by gas but by electricity: by 1935 even the gas company had to admit that the future of artificial lighting lay with electricity.

The centre, *c.* 1935–9: a view looking up Colston Street towards the City Council-owned Colston Hall, after the building of Radiant House and before tram services from the centre finished in 1939. The Victorian commercial block on the corner of Colston Street and Colston Avenue was demolished in May 1970 to make way for Colston Tower.

The centre, *c.* 1955: a post-war view of the centre showing the bland elongated roundabout landscaped in 1949 over the section of the Frome culverted between 1938 and 1940. The row of eighteenth- and nineteenth-century buildings on the north side of the centre, which planners in the 1940s had considered unworthy of a city centre, survived, although the Hippodrome lost its revolving dome in 1964.

The centre, *c.* 1965. Traffic roars around the municipal lawns and flower beds of the large traffic island on the centre – not a place of repose but just an obstacle to be crossed by pedestrians (right) as quickly as possible. Modern offices are already changing the cityscape – and the Robinson building rises above the buildings in Baldwin Street. The handsome Atlas and Sun Life building on the corner of Clare Street – a fine example of Edwardian baroque commercial architecture – was replaced in 1971 by a bland office block.

Bridgehead, 24 April 1968. Taken from the Bristol & West building, one of the new city centre landmarks of the 1960s, this view features several important post-war changes to this part of the centre: the landscaping at the head of the Frome with the statue of Neptune, completed in 1949; the Council House presiding over a flat and treeless College Green; and on the right the monolithic block of Gaunt's House, Bristol's first post-war office block, obscuring the tower of the Lord Mayor's chapel. Mid-'60s offices face College Green. The site of St Augustine-the-Less is a patch of derelict land, while the presence of a catamaran in St Augustine's Reach points to the future leisure role of the Floating Harbour.

CHAPTER THIRTEEN

RETAILING & VICTUALLING

In 1952 there were 7,159 shops in Bristol, one for every sixty-two people in the city. This number embraced a wide range of retailing businesses – from large prestigious department stores such as Baker, Baker & Co. to small corner shops. Roughly one seventh of the total were located in the city centre and reflected the city's role as a regional shopping centre. Another two thousand or so shops were located on the busy main roads leading out of the city, forming six important district shopping centres for the suburbs. They were located on Whiteladies Road including Cotham Hill; Gloucester Road including Cheltenham Road and Filton Road; Stapleton Road and Fishponds Road; Old Market and West Street, extending eastwards to Lawrence Hill and Church Road; Wells Road and Bedminster, with the largest number of shops in North Street followed by East Street and West Street. They contained a comprehensive range of shops including chain stores, banks and building society branches.

Smaller shopping centres were also spread across the suburbs: in Shirehampton, Clifton, Westbury-on-Trym and elsewhere; these were also self-contained shopping centres and included banks and post offices. Scattered throughout the city – particularly in the older suburban districts – small rows of shops and public houses were found, catering for the essential needs of residents in the immediate locality and often characterised by strong personal relationships between shopkeeper and customer. The shops in Whitehouse Street, Bedminster, before the war were a typical example: in 1939 there were two greengrocers, a butcher, boot repairer, a newsagent, grocer's shop, a fried fish shop, and a lamp and oil dealer as well as several general stores. The range, type and distribution of shops in Bristol underwent several important changes during this period, reflecting national changes in retailing – the rise of the chain stores, for example, and adapting to changes in consumer demand in a period of rising standards of living: in the 1920s and 1930s the number of electrical stores and car dealers increased at the expense of some traditional trades such as saddlery, which lost business as the city's horse population declined.

The larger department stores – with the obvious exception of Woolworths where before the war nothing cost more than 6*d* – emphasised their exclusiveness and quality with opulent interiors and enforced a rigid dress code on their staff. In the 1930s assistants employed by Cole & Pottow, high class gentlemen's outfitters in Park Street, changed their attire according to the seasons: in spring they wore a lounge suit with buttonhole; in summer white flannels and a boater; in the autumn they wore plus-fours and a trilby; and in winter a black coat and waistcoat, pin-striped trousers and either a bowler hat or homburg. The shop fronts often incorporated the latest ideas on shop design and advertising: chrome, plate glass and neon lights in the 1930s, large plastic fascias in the 1950s and 1960s.

The smaller shops, in contrast, were often conservative in appearance and preserved late Victorian or Edwardian shop fronts and interiors with lots of tiles, polished brass, wrought-iron work and mosaic floors in the entrance. Typically they were small, family-run concerns and many continued in business over several generations. The furnishings and counter equipment – even the smells – of the different types of shops gave them a distinctive atmosphere and character of their own: bacon waiting to be sliced was the predominant smell in grocery stores, blended, perhaps, with the sweet aroma of biscuits on open display in tins; the tiled interiors and smell of fresh sawdust characterised butchers' shops; while shoe repair shops were permeated with the strong smell of shoe polish and leather. The radio sets, gramophones and, from the 1950s, television sets filled the interior of electrical repair shops with the unmistakable smell emanating from large quantities of bakelite. The interiors of old fashioned chemists' shops – and there were several surviving in the 1960s – in Old Market, West Mall, Clifton and Blackboy Hill, for example – were lined with shelves filled with onion-shaped carboys, large glass bottles used for liquids and cylindrical bottles for solids, known, from their shape, as 'shop rounds'. Ironmongers' shops provided a wide range of household goods and offered a range of practical services such as the installation and repair of items and home decorating; they also had their own distinctive character, with galvanised ware displayed outside on the street and inside a strong smell of paraffin, glue and linseed oil. Many goods were sold loose: nails were sold by the pound and cement and plaster were also sold by weight; similarly, grocers sold many provisions loose. The scoops and counter scales of various kinds used to handle the goods were, in many cases, supplied by the Bristol firm W. Parnall & Co., who before the war had large premises in Victoria Street; they also supplied other shop fittings such as cash tills, display stands and cabinets and window blinds.

Retailing demanded specialised knowledge and skill that could only be acquired through a lengthy apprenticeship. Young assistants in clothes shops would be trained to measure and cut clothes and dress windows. In the ironmongery and hardware business the apprentices would be expected to familiarise themselves with the enormous range of small fixtures and fittings, lamp parts, plumbers' sundries, varnishes and paints. Apprentices in the shoe repair trade would be trained in leather-working techniques using specialised tools, while in the grocery trade assistants would learn to taste and blend teas, slice ham and learn about cheese and other foodstuffs. Shop assistants worked long hours and often on low wages, although many had a half day off on Wednesdays when many shops closed at 1.00 pm. Several small traders provided a delivery service. Besides the daily visit of the milkman, bakers often delivered daily while grocers, greengrocers and butchers made weekly deliveries. All the major retailing trades had their own associations which provided a range of services, including representation to manufacturers, suppliers and to relevant government bodies, and supplied insurance, legal advice and information on wages and holidays.

Shops belonging to the Bristol and District Co-operative Society were widely distributed across Bristol and formed an important and distinctive form of retailing in the city. The society was founded in 1884 by a group of trade unionists with the objective of sharing the profits made through the production and sale of the 'necessaries of life' with members – the consumers – and not just a few shopkeepers. Starting with a shop in St Paul's, branches were opened in Hotwells and Lawrence Hill, and by the mid-1930s there were fifty-two grocery, confectionery and greengrocery branches in Bristol, seven drapery, clothing and boot branches, two hardware and furnishing shops and nineteen butchery branches. There were also shops in nearby towns such as Weston-super-Mare and Clevedon. In 1918 new central premises were established in Castle Street, which opened as a department store in 1930. In 1938 co-operative stores in Britain accounted for 10 per cent of retail trade but the societies saw their role in wider terms. 'Co-operation', it was affirmed in the Bristol members' guide for 1934, ' is not merely producing and shopkeeping, it is a method of life.' The Bristol society, for example, had a Women's Guild which educated members in the principles of the movement and on other social issues affecting everyday life. For the majority of members, however, the greatest benefit of society membership was the payment of the dividend – the 'divi' – of 1s 8d for every £1 spent in the shops.

Before the war the most important and prestigious shops were located in two major shopping centres: the first was the Wine Street/Castle Street area, including Union Street, Dolphin Street, Mary-le-Port Street and Peter Street, where 218 shops were located in 1939. The second major concentration, consisting of 193 shops in 1939, followed the main route to Clifton from College Green to Queens Road via Park Street. In both centres clothes, boot and shoe shops accounted for almost 40 per cent of the total, with food and drink shops the second largest category. Miscellaneous stores included radio shops, such as J. & M. Stone who had shops in Wine Street and Castle Street, Kendall's umbrella shop in Union Street and Halford's cycle store in Castle Street. Two large Bristol department stores – Jones & Co. and Baker, Baker & Co. – had premises in Wine Street where the most exclusive shops were found, and by the 1930s several important multiple traders – Woolworths, Boots, Burtons and Marks & Spencer – were located in Castle Street. The larger chains increased in importance between the wars: nationally between 1920 and 1939 the larger companies with more than 200 branches or more increased from 10,942 to 21,283. The Wine Street/Castle Street shopping centre was busy through the week until the early evening and later on Saturdays, when the shops stayed open until 9.00 pm. On a Saturday night the streets were thronged with people looking for bargains, particularly fresh food (fish, fruit and vegetables) being sold off cheap. Barrow boys, selling fruit and vegetables mostly, were an essential part of the scene with their entertaining banter, their handcarts illuminated by candle lamps on dark evenings.

Enemy bombing destroyed the Wine Street/Castle Street shopping centre: a total of 487 shops were lost in the central area and many traders had to find new premises quickly: an immediate effect was to enhance the importance of the city's radial shopping centres. The City Council ruled out the option of rebuilding shops in Wine Street and Castle Street and instead resolved to develop a new shopping precinct at Broadmead. Despite strong opposition from many local traders and shoppers, the City Council pressed ahead with plans for Broadmead, and the 1950s saw the development of a new shopping precinct which consolidated the hold of the multi-traders at the expense of locally based businesses; moreover, Broadmead never recaptured the atmosphere of the pre-war city centre shopping area. A few shops in Castle Street survived the blitz and lingered on for a while: the Bristol Co-operative Society's headquarters continued in business until the building of Fairfax House in about 1960, and the last shop in Castle Street was Burtons, which survived until 1964.

The pattern of shops in the suburbs also changed in the post-war period. New shopping centres were built on the new post-war housing estates in the 1950s, in Lawrence Weston, Henbury, Stockwood, Withywood and Hartcliffe. At the same time clearances in the older suburbs, such as in Redcliff, parts of Bedminster and St Phillips Marsh, resulted in the closure of many small shops. Thus the small shops in Whitehouse Street, Bedminster, which had thrived before the war, had mostly gone by 1950 as the area was cleared to make way for a light industrial and trading estate. From the late 1950s the small shopkeepers, particularly grocers and general corner shops, found themselves facing a new rival – the supermarket. The development of large self-service stores was a gradual one which began in the 1950s, with some of the larger

Shop window display, Mumford's grocery store, 11 High Street, Westbury-on-Trym, 1951. This window arrangement featuring coffee was inspired by Alma Cogan's song 'Coffee in the Morning'. It was entered for a shop window competition organised by the Bristol & District Grocers' & Provision Dealers' Association which represented the grocery trade in Bristol from 1891 until 1992, when it was dissolved following a decline in membership.

grocery companies such as the Bristol Co-operative Society turning to this method of retailing. Supermarkets first acquired a separate entry in Kelly's Directory in 1964. By the end of the decade there were nearly sixty supermarkets in Bristol and they had successfully gained a foothold in most of the city's suburban shopping centres, some of them occupying former cinemas, such as the Cabot in Filton and the Ritz in Brislington, which found a new lease of life as a Kwik Save store. In 1969 there were seventeen Co-operative supermarkets in Bristol, twenty-three belonging to Gateway and a smaller number of self-service stores owned by Tesco, International, Spar and Fine Fare. The small independently owned stores could not compete with supermarket prices – and, perhaps, the novelty and convenience of shopping in supermarkets – and began to decline in numbers. Notwithstanding the expansion of Bristol between 1920 and 1969, numbers of butchers and grocers – two staple food shops – declined over this period: in 1920 there were some 550 grocers (excluding Bristol Co-operative Society Shops) in Bristol, but by 1969 the figure had dropped to about 420; while numbers of butchers' shops decreased slightly, from roughly 270 in 1920 to about 250 in 1969.

In 1920 there were 371 public houses in Bristol. Some were of considerable antiquity: the Shakespeare in Temple Street was claimed as Bristol's oldest hostelry, possibly dating to 1636. Other old inns included the Greyhound Hotel in Broadmead, the Hatchet Inn in Frogmore Street and the Llandoger Trow, where Daniel Defoe apparently met Alexander Selkirk, the inspiration for Robinson Crusoe and also the model for the Spy-glass in Robert Louis Stevenson's Treasure Island. Tucked away in St Thomas Lane between nineteenth-century industrial premises was the Seven Stars, a notorious haunt of slave traders in the eighteenth century. There were many other public houses in the city centre which were in existence before 1800. In the nineteenth century the public house was an important place of working-class entertainment, and in districts such as Barton Hill, Easton and Bedminster there were many public houses built in the second half of the nineteenth century. The Llandoger Trow was one of just a handful of free houses in the city; the great majority were tied houses belonging to George's, Bristol's largest brewer, although Ushers and Simonds also owned pubs in the city. George's came to dominate brewing in Bristol in the late nineteenth century through a series of take-overs of competitors. Their expansion in the early twentieth century was also based on the sale of bottled beers, which were sold in the city's numerous off-licences. The firm's biggest rival, the Bristol United Brewery, was absorbed in 1956 and its brewery in Lewins Mead closed down; then in 1961 George's was taken over by Courage. Many public houses were lost in the blitz and many more were victims of post-war clearances when small street corner pubs and off-licences were swept away. Pubs were at first excluded from the pre-war council estates; residents of the new houses in Sea Mills, for example, had to walk to

Westbury-on-Trym or Shirehampton before finding a pub. Nevertheless, after the war public houses were established in areas of new housing. By 1969 the number of public houses in Bristol had increased to 430, although this was a lower density than fifty years earlier.

Market entrance from All Saints Lane, 1930s: an atmospheric scene as sunshine streams into this narrow passageway which runs from Corn Street to St Nicholas Street. The tower of St Nicholas' church is in the distance beyond the Crown public house. The Crown was one of the few free houses in the city and is advertising draught Bass. The Market was designed by Samuel Glascodine and opened in 1745 for the sale of meat and vegetables; it remained in use as a wholesale fruit market until 1968 when a new one in St Phillips was opened.

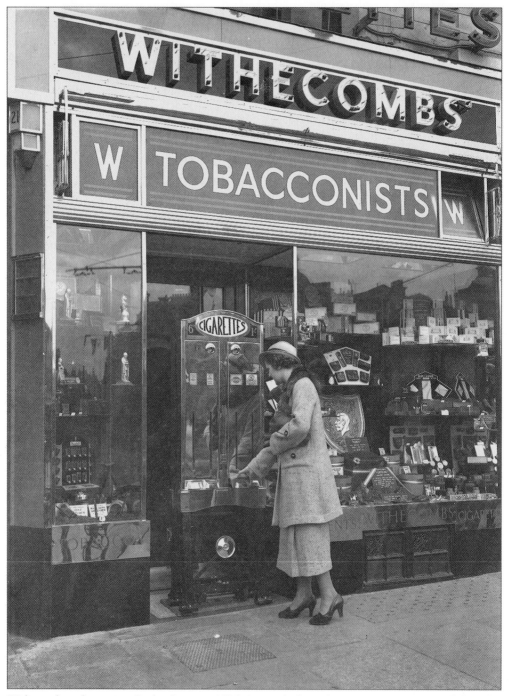

Withecombs, tobacconists, Bridge Street, c. 1936. A smartly dressed young woman wearing a fashionable stole around her neck buys a packet of twenty cigarettes – either Wills Gold Flake or Players Navy Cut – for 1s from a coin slot machine outside Withecombs shop in Bridge Street. Prominent in the window display is a commemorative shield marking the 1935 Jubilee of King George V. This was a boom time for the tobacco industry and retailers: between 1928 and 1940 *per capita* consumption of tobacco and cigarettes practically doubled.

Willsons, ladies outfitters, Castle Street from Cock and Bottle Lane, late 1930s. In the heart of the pre-war shopping centre, Wilsons store, established in 1933, advertises new spring fashions; there is a hairdressing salon on the first floor and a restaurant and cafe on the lower ground floor. The main sign is in sans serif lettering, which became fashionable in the 1930s, and is illuminated by neon lights. Pre-war Castle Street contained several other clothes shops, including Stuckey's outfitters on the left-hand corner of Cock and Bottle Lane. Several major chain stores including Boots, British Home Stores, Burtons, Marks & Spencer and Woolworths were also located in Castle Street; and the Bristol Co-operative Society had its head offices there.

The Lower Arcade, Broadmead, *c*. 1950. A blind man passes the Broadmead entrance to the Lower Arcade, designed by James Foster and built in 1825. The arcade runs between the Horsefair and Broadmead and was threatened by the post-war plans for the new Broadmead shopping centre, but the planned demolition was reversed in 1947 following protests from the Council for the Protection of Ancient Bristol and others.

Broadmead, looking towards the Odeon and Nelson Street, late 1950s. The Dolcis shop has been claimed as the most imaginative modern shop in the new centre: the façade, according to John Punter, was 'a sophisticated play between transparent planes that was especially striking at night'. Before the war Dolcis had its shop was on the corner of Wine Street and Dolphin Street.

Lewis's Department Store, the Horsefair, *c.* 1958. This department store of startling white Portland stone was built on the site of St James's churchyard and designed by Sir Percy Thomas. The store, the largest in Bristol, opened on 26 September 1958 and became an important part of the Broadmead shopping centre.

New shops on the corner of Broadmead and Union Street, September 1953. The premises of Swears and Wells, furriers, was designed by the City Architect in the restrained modern style that he was promoting for the whole of Broadmead. The Woolworths store was designed by the company's own architect, who adopted a more futuristic façade above set-back display windows, while H. Samuel, next door, chose a façade with recessed curtain walling within a Bath stone frame. Before the war, H. Samuel and Swears and Wells were located in Wine Street and Woolworths in Castle Street.

Park Street, *c.* 1935. Rising from College Green to Clifton, Park Street was one of the city's principal shopping streets with a reputation for high-quality shops. Barr's saddlers shop on the left was soon to be demolished to make way for the site of the new Council House on College Green.

Park Street, 1950s. Originally entitled 'Rainy Day Reflections', this photograph provides a surprising double image of the Wills building reflected in a shop window. Designed by Sir George Oatley, the Wills building was opened by King George V and Queen Mary on 9 June 1925.

Queens Road, *c.* 1930: a pre-war scene of this up-market shopping street. Maggs' sign partially covers the first-floor windows of the elegant Royal Parade built in the 1850s (see *Bristol 1850–1919*, page 75). Established in about 1857 as bedding manufacturers and house furnishers, Maggs & Co. opened its department store in the Royal Parade, Queens Road, in about 1895, selling a wide range of goods including furniture, electrical goods, ironmongery, gardening tools, china and glass. Duck Son & Pinker was started in Bath in 1848 and in Bristol in 1886. The Bristol branch was originally located at 13 Queens Road and subsequently at 1 Royal Parade, where they had extensive showrooms on three floors stocked with pianos, harmoniums and organs. The Queens Road premises were blitzed during the war. The building on the right is the headquarters of Lennards Ltd, boot and shoe makers; it was completely destroyed in the Blitz.

Interior view of the entrance hall of the headquarters of Lennards Ltd, 1923. Established in 1877, the company claimed to be one of the largest shoe businesses in the British Empire with over two hundred branches, fifteen of which were in Bristol. Shoes were sold worldwide by mail order from Bristol. With its corner clock tower, the building was a prominent landmark in Queen's Road until it was bombed in the war. The company had a shoe factory in Northampton and its own holiday and convalescent home for staff at Weston-super-Mare.

The showroom windows of Beacon House, Queens Road, shine brightly in the gathering dusk – signalling the new era of domestic electricity, *c*. 1933. Hitherto, Gardiner Sons & Co. Ltd, established in 1860, had concentrated largely on architectural foundry work and wholesale ironmongery sold from their premises in Nelson Street, but the opening of these showrooms in 1933 represented a major shift towards retail trading. An advertisement in Kellys Directory for 1933 invited the customer to 'inspect these super showrooms' containing 'a splendid selection' of household ironmongery, garden tools and ornaments, fireplaces and cooking stoves, bathroom fittings and the newest electrical goods'. The building began life as the Queens Hotel in October 1854. Gardiner's sold Beacon House in 1957 when they moved to Broad Plain, and the building was subsequently occupied by Taylors, Debenhams and Habitat.

The red telephone box was then a relatively new addition to the street scene. Designed by the architect Sir Giles Gilbert Scott and first introduced in London in 1926, this type of kiosk with several variations became widely established in Bristol and elsewhere during the 1930s. Tramlines in the road reflect the light of the electric street lamp, first introduced in the city in 1893.

Bristol Co-operative Society butcher's shop, 44 Chelsea Road, Easton, *c.* 1936. The Bristol Co-operative Society was founded in 1884 to give members a share in the profits on the sale of a wide range of goods and each member was paid a dividend based on the value of their purchases. The Society ran nineteen butchery branches in Bristol in the mid-1930s; a co-operative grocery store was located next door to this butcher's shop.

C. Allen & Co., motor agents, 159 Whiteladies Road, *c.* 1936. Smartly attired attendants in white overalls and peaked caps are photographed alongside Armstrong Siddeley saloon cars. C. Allen & Sons were established at these premises from about 1934 but had gone by 1947. The 1920s and 1930s saw a marked growth in retail outlets catering for the increasing numbers of motorists. Barclays Bank on the corner of Burlington Road is seen on the extreme left.

Aitken's shoe repair shop, 6 Abbotsford Road, Cotham, mid-1920s. This business was started in 1919 by Edward (Ted) Aitken who then opened a second shop in Sandy Park, Brislington, which continued until his death in 1941. The business was continued by his son, Ivor, in Cotham Hill until 1985. The shop window is crowded with advertisements for Cherry Blossom and Nugget shoe polish, and displays of inner soles, heels and other shoe accessories.

Connett's, drapers, 116 Whiteladies Road, 1920s. Ladies' underwear, lace and ties can be identified in the window display of this shop, which was established by William George Connett in about 1908. A second shop was opened at 408 Gloucester Road, Horfield, in about 1925. The Whiteladies Road shop was still in business in 1969.

Shops in Syme's Avenue, Hartcliffe, late 1950s. Bristol's post-war council estates acquired their own local shopping centres, with shops similar in design to these in Hartcliffe. The ice cream van belongs to Verrechia, who started selling ice cream in Bristol in 1925 and is credited with introducing the ice cream van to Britain.

Grocer's shop, *c.* 1947. The customer is ready with her book of coupons. Rationing had been introduced during the war and remained in force until 1954. There was a worsening for the domestic consumer after 1945: bread, which had not been rationed at any time during the war, was rationed between July 1946 and July 1947 and potatoes at the end of 1947.

G. Thorne, grocer and tobacconist, on the corner of Muller Road and Stapleton Road, Eastville, 1960s. Brook Bond, TyPhoo and Lyons Tea are advertised in the window along with Wall's ice cream, Heinz baked beans and Birds Eye foods. The thirteen-arch railway viaduct in the background carried the line of the former Midland Railway to Avonmouth, and was demolished in 1968 to make way for the construction of the M32 motorway.

Park Side filling and service station, Stapleton Road, Eastville, mid-1960s. Two female petrol attendants in overalls chat in the doorway of the shop between serving Cleveland petrol (a subsidiary of Esso) to motorists at prices ranging from 5s 2½d to 5s 9d a gallon. For 2d extra the customer received a double strip of 'pink stamps'; these, like the rival 'Green Shield' stamps, were collected in books which could be exchanged for gifts. From the 1970s many small petrol stations such as this fell before competition from larger 'self-service' garages owned by the petrol companies.

The Llandoger Trow, King Street, 1930s. Occupying the right-hand house of a group of five gabled timber-framed houses built in 1664, the Llandoger Trow can be traced to 1775; the name refers to the flat-bottomed trows or boats built at Llandogo on the Wye that sailed across the Bristol Channel to Welsh Back. The two end houses were destroyed in the blitz and the pub now occupies all three surviving houses, but in this pre-war view the next house is occupied by F.C. Brummel, plumber and electrician. In the 1920s he is listed in trade directories as a plumber and gas fitter, but, moving with the times, was advertising his services as an electrician by the 1930s.

The Railway Inn, Stapleton Road, 1930s. Stapleton Road railway station opened in 1863 and the public house first appears in local trade directories for 1867; in the 1930s it was one of over 900 licensed premises in Bristol and the surrounding area belonging to George's Brewery. There are thirteen identical buff earthenware chimney pots on the two stacks.

The Royal Hotel on the corner of Gloucester Road and Clayton Street, Avonmouth, 1930s. This attractive row of late nineteenth-century shops including the hotel was built in the Domestic Revival Style with attractive gables and moulded brick chimneys; the steps surrounding the block were apparently intended as a flood barrier.

The Rising Sun, corner of Lower Castle Street and Ellbroad Street, c. 1950. This public house is listed in Mathew's Bristol Directory for 1794; having been rebuilt around the turn of the century it was demolished in 1954.

CHAPTER FOURTEEN

HOUSING & DOMESTIC LIFE

In 1920 most people in Bristol lived in privately owned rented accommodation. Home ownership was rare, and although Bristol's first council houses had been built in Chapel Street and Mina Road in about 1901, working-class people lived mostly in Victorian terraced houses located in the industrial suburbs or occupied rooms in tenements, many of slum standard, close to the city centre. Houses were gas lit; cooking still commonly took place on coal burning kitchen ranges – although the use of gas cookers was rapidly increasing; and a brick and iron wash-copper was used for the weekly wash: this task, traditionally allotted to Mondays, was hard, labour-intensive work. The majority of smaller homes had no bathroom or inside toilet. Middle-class homes were larger and better equipped, but their occupants were having to adjust to a shortage of servants following the end of the First World War. Early issues of *Homes and Gardens*, first published in 1919 and catering for a middle-class audience, featured labour-saving domestic arrangements for the 'servantless house'. Over the next fifty years the way people lived in Bristol changed radically as a revolution occurred in the quality of housing and living standards.

A fundamental shift in attitude towards the provision of working-class housing occurred towards the end of the First World War. By 1918 there was, nationwide, an acute shortage of housing: it was clear that private developers would not be able to supply houses in the quantity – and of the quality expected – at rents that the average working-class family could afford. So the government intervened, and in 1919 the Liberal Minister of Health, Sir Christopher Addison, introduced a Housing Act which required local authorities to survey their housing needs and make good the deficiency with the assistance of a generous government subsidy. Anticipating the legislation, Bristol City Council established a Housing Extensions & Town Planning Committee in March 1918 and quickly formed a plan of action. Village suburbs were to be created across the city, and before the end of the year land was purchased in Sea Mills, Shirehampton and Knowle. In 1919 Bristol's first council house built under the terms of the Addison Act was completed in Beechen Drive, Fishponds.

A total of 1,189 Addison houses were built in Bristol. In 1919, however, the housing shortage in Bristol was reckoned to stand at 5,000 dwellings, so this first wave of council building fell short of meeting the city's housing needs. Nevertheless, the new estates in Fishponds, Sea Mills and Bedminster represented a complete break with the past and expressed a totally new approach to working-class housing. Local authority control of the Victorian working-class suburb was largely restricted to ensuring that new houses were sanitary, but little else. They were not planned but grew piecemeal, according to the vagaries of speculative development by small builders and other entrepreneurs. The new council estates were, in complete contrast, planned environments, designed and controlled by the Council; this was not simply a policy of rehousing, it was also institutionalised social engineering creating a new pattern of life for thousands of people. The estates were conceived as self-contained communities with churches, schools and shops, although public houses were at first excluded. Their layout followed the guidelines set by the Tudor Walters report published in 1918, which drew heavily on the garden city ideal introduced at the end of the nineteenth century. The Tudor Walters Committee criticised the typical late nineteenth-century working-class suburb for the monotony of the long, parallel rows of houses, and the houses themselves – for their narrow frontages and rear projections which obstructed light and air at the back. Instead, the new council developments aimed to create self-sufficient cottage homes in low-density garden suburbs, and following the recommendations of the Tudor Walters Report there were to be no more than twelve houses to an acre. The first estates in Fishponds and Sea Mills incorporated a mixture of different house types; rows of four were combined with semi-detached houses, designed in a simple cottage style and employing traditional building materials. The interior plan of the houses also varied: the basic distinction was between houses with a parlour and those without; all houses, however, had a scullery and all were equipped with a bath. The houses were given generous sized plots with gardens front and back. While providing a relaxed setting, the idea was also to encourage the tenants to grow vegetables. Some of the houses were laid out in attractive crescents – as at Sea Mills, Fishponds and Knowle Park – avoiding the monotony associated with the long straight rows of Victorian terraces. In Knowle, Broad Walk – laid out from the mid-1920s – was designed as a wide, tree-lined boulevard: the contrast with the older inner city suburbs could not have been greater.

In 1923 Neville Chamberlain, Minister of Health in the new Conservative government, passed another Housing Act which aimed to encourage building by private enterprise. This Act constituted a complete reversal of the 1919 policy of encouraging local authorities to become major providers of working-class housing. Only 1,655 council houses were built in Bristol under this scheme, although the subsidy did stimulate private house building. Another change in government – this time the first Labour administration – resulted in yet another Housing Act, introduced by J. Wheatley, the new Minister of Health, which restored the local authority subsidy for house building. It remained in operation until 1933 and is generally regarded as the most successful of the inter-war housing measures. In Bristol 7,114 houses were financed under the Wheatley subsidy; they were generally smaller than the earlier houses, elevations were simpler and there were more short terraces in place of crescents, as building in straight rows was less expensive. Non-traditional building methods were tried, including metal frame construction – such as the 'Dorman Long'-type houses built in Sylvan Way, Sea Mills, in 1926. Experiments were also made with concrete houses, and in Knowle Park with all-metal houses, which suffered from condensation.

The new council estates, however, did not supply the needs of the poorer sections of the working class. Rents remained high and sub-letting was forbidden upon pain of eviction. As a result, only the higher paid worker could afford them, leaving the mass of poorer workers living in older properties – some of them slums and many located near the centre. By the late 1920s attention was turning to their plight, and in 1930 a new Housing Act was passed which introduced a subsidy for the clearance of slums and the re-housing of the families displaced. The scheme was delayed by the economic crisis of 1931 but in 1933, following the passing of another Housing Act, Bristol City Council approved a programme for the clearance of 2,900 slum properties. These were located chiefly in parts of Bedminster, St Phillips, St Judes and other inner city areas; following demolition, the occupants were rehoused in new council houses erected in Bedminster and Knowle.

By 1939 the occupants of 3,500 slum clearance houses had been rehoused. Economies in standards continued: there were more of the cheaper non-parlour houses, for example, and the estates containing the rehoused slum families, as in Knowle West, came to be seen in the popular mind as 'rough', as opposed to the older estates such as Sea Mills, which were perceived as 'respectable'. Nevertheless, the former slum dwellers were probably unaware of such fine distinctions: what mattered to them was the huge improvement in their environment: compare the scene in Weare's Buildings illustrated on page 231 with the spacious setting of the houses in Wordsworth Road in Horfield on page 240. One former occupant of a slum recalls her excitement as a young child of seven moving to a new council house in Knowle West in 1935. Her family had occupied two rooms at the top of a four-storey tenement in Houlton Street, St Judes, where there was one toilet in the back yard for all the residents. The move represented an almost imaginable improvement in living standards. They now had an entire house to themselves. The house was still lit by gas but it had a bathroom, whereas in St Judes they had used a galvanised zinc bath, hung on a nail in the yard, which was carried inside and used in front of the fire. The kitchen was provided with a gas boiler which made the task of the weekly wash a lot easier. They had a garden – space for children to play in – and there was plenty of greenery and trees; compared with St Judes, Knowle West was like the countryside. The division between work and home which had characterised the Victorian and Edwardian middle-class suburbs was now extended to the working-class suburb. Living on a new council estate on the edge of the city left many residents with a considerably longer journey to work, and the benefits of the new, well-equipped home had to be weighed against the sense of isolation which some residents clearly felt. Life on the new estates could be dull. The provision of amenities such as shops and leisure facilities often lagged far behind the building of the homes: there were no shops in Sea Mills, for example, until 1929.

Between 1919 and 1939 some 36,000 houses were built in Bristol: 14,500 of these were council houses but about 60 per cent were built by private builders responding to the demand from middle-class house buyers, the 'owner-earners' as one 1930s Bristol builder called them. The middle class expanded markedly after 1920, particularly because of the increase in non-manual occupations in management, teaching, administrative and clerical work. The new recruits were keen to demonstrate their arrival by assuming a lifestyle which separated them from the respectable working-class origins from which they had, in many cases, risen. Their predominant aspiration was to own a house, and in the 1920s and 1930s low interest rates coupled with the easier availability of mortgages, rising real wages, and falling building costs after 1930, brought home ownership within the reach of many for the first time. Home ownership was encouraged by the expansion of building societies, such as the Bristol & West, who supplied affordable mortgages, while the access to the house market was provided by an ever increasing number of estate agents.

Middle-class suburban development represented, above all, by the pebble-dashed, three bedroom 'semi', was widespread across Bristol but particularly extensive in the north-west of the city, which, based on Victorian and Edwardian building in Sneyd Park, Redland and Henleaze, was already established as a desirable area. The estates built in the 1920s and 1930s continued the outward movement towards the edge of the city where residents could create a respectable and secure environment free of the undesirable associations of city life. They consisted mostly of speculative ventures by builders who bought land from country landowners: the Harfords, for example, owners of the Blaise Castle Estate, Henbury, until 1926, sold land in Westbury-on-Trym for residential development between the wars; Falcondale Road, a mid-1930s development, was named after their residence near Lampeter in Wales. The builders aimed to provide low-density houses (usually no more than twelve per acre) in a variety of house styles – providing an element of individuality and a range of prices. Thus Kellaway Avenue, Horfield, laid out in 1920, was subsequently filled with a mixed development of houses and bungalows. The latter became popular in the 1920s, offering small yet detached accommodation, ideal for older people.

Three estates in Stapleton, Stoke Bishop and Westbury-on-Trym, developed simultaneously by Stone & Co., Redland-based builders, in the mid-1930s when the building boom was at its height, illustrate the range of houses available. The cheapest were located on the Colston Estate in Stapleton overlooking Eastville Park, where three types of relatively plain semi-detached three bedroomed houses were available in 1936 from £565. Semis were also built on the Druid Stoke and Henbury Hill Estates, although several

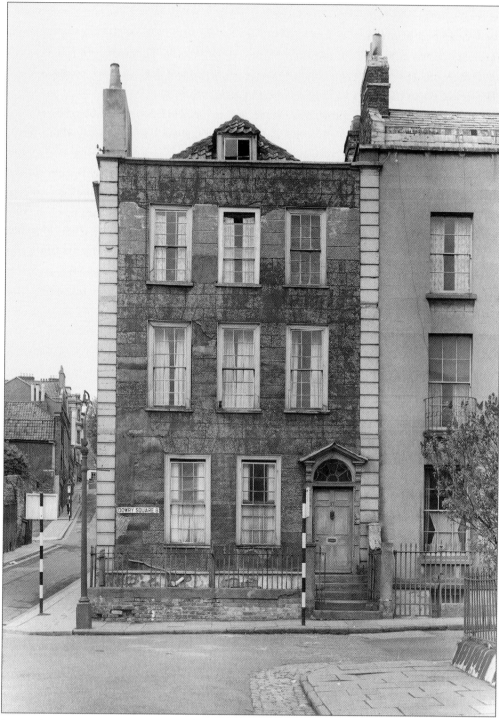

Dowry Square, May 1956. The City Council's 1952 Development Report calculated that there were 35,000 houses predating 1880 in the city, those in Dowry Square being some of the earliest. The houses in the square were built between 1720 and about 1750 to provide fashionable lodgings for visitors to the nearby Hotwells.

different designs of detached houses ranging in price from £975 to £1,500 were included. All the houses on the three estates were designed by Bristol architects, including Alec French and James & Meredith. Architectural embellishments increased with the price of the house. The façades of the Colston Estate were similar to council houses – apart from their two-storey bay window – but the more expensive designs on the other two estates contained a rich mixture of traditional motifs which characterised this house type all over Britain. Tile-hung walls, leaded casement windows and mock half-timbered gables drew on traditional vernacular – or cottage-style – architecture. The steeply pitched roof of the house in Falcondale Road illustrated on page 243 recalls the picturesque, fantasy designs of Blaise Hamlet by John Nash (1752–1835) less than 2 miles away. Gothic motifs such as embattled walls added to the variety and catered for the owner's wish for a home with individual character. Yet no amount of dressing up in retrospective styles could hide the essential 1930s character of these houses, with their often harsh red brickwork and grey pebble-dash. The building of a few houses in the modernistic International Style in Stoke Bishop at least introduced a note of originality of design, but their stark white walls, flat roofs and curved glass bay windows never won popular appeal.

The interior layout of the typical 1930s private house combined traditional values with modern requirements. The Victorian convention of segregated room use was maintained with the two principal ground-floor rooms serving as lounge and dining room. Separate access to these was provided from the hall, which, frequently panelled in oak, complemented the traditional house exterior and provided an appropriate backdrop to a display of antique or reproduction furniture, copper and brassware. Stairways were often traditional with turned balusters, but simpler designs which required less dusting became popular in the 1930s. Convenience within the home was important to this servantless middle class, larger than its Edwardian predecessor but also poorer, and labour-saving arrangements – especially in the kitchen – became an important consideration in their design. By the 1920s cooking over a coal-burning kitchen range was rapidly giving way to cooking by gas, which was cleaner and easier to use. In 1935 the Bristol Gas Company claimed to have 105,000 gas cookers in use in the city (in about 90 per cent of homes), and these were available either through hire purchase or cheap weekly rents. Gas boilers for doing the weekly wash were also widely adopted, replacing the coal-fired wash copper as seen in the scullery on page 239. However, by the early 1930s gas was facing stiff competition from electricity. Between the mid-1920s and the early 1930s electricity was laid in most streets in the city, and in 1929 a new large power station built by the City Council's Electric Department at Portishead was brought into use. The increase in the domestic consumption of electricity in Bristol was dramatic: in 1924 there were 14,397 users; by 1935 the figure had increased to 71,935 (over 63 per cent of all households). In 1929 a Bristol branch of the Electrical Association for Women was established, and in 1934 built an all-electric house in Stoke Bishop – in the modern style, appropriately – to demonstrate the potential of electricity in the home, its convenience and cleanliness. Notwithstanding the interest, locally and nationally, in this demonstration, the impact of electrical appliances was uneven: electric irons were readily adopted and vacuum cleaners were also popular, but the widespread use of electric cookers and washing machines had to wait until the 1950s.

House building came to a virtual standstill during the war, and the pre-war housing shortage was exacerbated by the destruction of 3,000 homes by enemy action. Temporary accommodation was provided by pre-fabricated houses; over 3,000 were erected in Ashton Vale, Sea Mills, Westbury-on Trym and elsewhere. While these proved popular with their occupants they were only ever intended as a temporary measure and the provision of new council housing was the City's top priority after 1945. Building soon resumed in the same spirit of optimism which surrounded official plans for the remodelling of the city centre. The break in the house building programme caused by the war gave planners the opportunity to review housing policy; they were guided by the findings of the Dudley Commission published in 1944, which like the earlier Tudor Walters Report reviewed existing housing types and made recommendations for future house building. The report was critical of the monotony of the typical pre-war council estate and recommended that a greater variety of house types was introduced. This criticism was held widely. The repetition of the same or very similar architectural units had created a dull, repetitive urban landscape, which, moreover, consisted of a single class. Achieving greater physical diversity in house types and mixing social groups were seen as vital to future developments, and these principles were embodied in the notion of the 'neighbourhood unit', which became a widely held planning concept after the war.

Neighbourhood units were perceived as self-contained communities including a wide mix of house types – and therefore social groups – supported by schools, libraries, health and recreational facilities and factories to provide local employment. In its first Development Plan published in 1952, the City Council asserted that sub-division of Bristol into neighbourhood units would foster 'a co-operative spirit between the social classes . . . to overcome the social and civic difficulties from which the large city suffers'. Adoption of the neighbourhood unit, therefore, represented more than a housing policy: the City was assuming responsibility for social planning – and while this had been a feature of council estate design ever since the idea of village suburbs was first mooted in 1918, post-war policy represented a far greater level of control over all Bristolians and their homes than had ever previously existed.

The neighbourhood unit principle was applied to all the new post-war housing estates at Henbury, Lawrence Weston, Lockleaze, Stockwood and Hartcliffe, and also to the redevelopment of older areas such as Barton Hill. A greater mix of house types characterised these areas, and included blocks and flats as well as prefabricated houses of steel and concrete, such as the 'Woolaway' houses built in Lawrence Weston and

Henbury in the early 1950s. A small number of flats had been built by the Council before the war in Hotwells, but the fashion for high-rise flats originated in the 1920s and 1930s among architects of the Modern Movement. One of the earliest post-war blocks in Bristol was St Peter's House, an eight-storey block of maisonettes on the corner of Hotwell and Jacobs Wells Road, which curiously combined traditional services behind a modern façade: each maisonette was heated by a coal fire fitted with a back boiler supplying heat to radiators in the two bedrooms. Each dwelling had a coal bunker off the kitchen, while massive chimney flues ran through the centre of the two main wings. Later blocks, built after the 1956 Clean Air Act, were designed with full central heating.

At Barton Hill the creation of a neighbourhood unit involved the construction of high-rise blocks from the mid-1950s while retaining some of the streets of Victorian terraced houses. The intention was to retain a sense of community, which clearly did not flourish within a tower block. The flats were ugly and jarring on the outside, and their occupants often felt a sense of isolation; without gardens, the flats were unsuitable for families with children. Nevertheless, blocks of flats continued to be built into the mid-1960s – at Redcliff, Lawrence Weston, Hartcliffe and Kingsdown – but mounting criticism of their social (and visual) shortcomings and the structural failure of the Ronan Point block in London in 1968 caused a strong reaction against further building of this type of accommodation. In practice, the idea of the neighbourhood unit fell far short of its original objectives. Arguably, the greatest success was achieved in Henbury where the visual and social impact of the Council-built houses and flats in the 1950s was diluted by the existence of an historic village centre, and where extensive private house building occurred in the 1960s. Lawrence Weston, Lockleaze and particularly Hartcliffe failed, however, to achieve the diverse social mix originally projected, and ironically these estates came to be particularly associated with those social problems that the neighbourhood unit was intended to solve. Their isolation – social and geographical – has, nevertheless, created over time a strong sense of community on these estates, notwithstanding the very real social problems which exist.

By the end of 1972, 33,461 council homes had been built – twice the number built before the war – housing about 40 per cent of Bristol's population. Home ownership continued to increase, reflecting improved standards of living, and many new private homes were built in the late 1950s and 1960s. Across Bristol, from Stockwood to Henbury, housing developments by large national companies, such as Wimpey, took place. Exterior design easily distinguished them from council property: white painted weatherboarding or cedarwood cladding in imitation of Scandinavian style were popular – so, too, were dormer windows – and owing to the widespread adoption of central heating, chimneys all but disappeared. Acknowledging the rapid increase in car ownership, most had a garage. Privately built post-war houses were often smaller than their pre-war counterparts, but in responding to increased informality in family life the open-plan interior was widely adopted. Generally, in terms of space and amenity standards, the gap between the 'middle class' and 'working-class' home, which had been particularly marked in the early twentieth century, had considerably narrowed. Most people had benefited from the huge improvements, therefore, which occurred between the 1920s and 1960s.

Weare's Buildings, Bedminster, 17 November 1931. The photograph provides a fascinating record of a 1930s slum: many of the residents have come outside their front doors to be in the photograph taken by the City Council shortly before demolition; women and children predominate – the men being at work, or just out. With Hope Square, which ran close to the back of the row on the left, these Georgian houses of about 1810 to 1820 formed a small self-contained world, hemmed in by adjoining factories and reached only by a narrow passage-way from York Road, off to the right. By 1930 they ranked among the worst slum properties in the city, and were condemned in 1931 in accordance with the 1930 Housing Act; the inhabitants were rehoused in new council houses in Bedminster and Knowle.

They were two-up, two-down dwellings: two bedrooms were reached by a narrow twisting stairway located between the front parlour and the kitchen. The kitchens had a range with an oven and opened on to a tiny back yard – 9 ft by 5 ft – which contained a sink and cold water tap open to the elements. On one side of the yard, housed in a small, single-storey lean-to, was a WC without a flush, and on the other side was another small structure housing a washing copper. The yards and outhouses of Hope Square backed on to those of Weare's Buildings, so that the rear walls of the two rows of houses were only about 10 ft apart, providing little light and poor ventilation. While there were narrow gardens at the front with valuable space for drying washing, they, too, must have seen little sun and appear to contain old junk and wooden hutches. Added to the almost perpetual gloom in which the occupants lived, they also had to tolerate the smells at close quarters from two of the most obnoxious industries conceivable – leather tanning and the manufacture of glue from animal bones. No wonder the incidence of mortality and disease was high in this little quarter.

Dereliction and squalor at the rear of eighteenth-century houses, May 1956. The first three houses on the left face on to Hope Square – see opposite top – while the front of the two houses on the right of the picture are on Granby Hill. All these houses survive.

Hope Square, May 1956. The late eighteenth-century houses overlooking the square, seen here, joined the row of houses on Granby Hill at an acute angle (i.e. less than ninety degrees) with the result that the windows of the two houses in the corner, just visible on the extreme left, look into each other. The houses on the square were subsequently refurbished, but most of those on the Granby Hill side were replaced with private flats.

'Bin day' in Langton Street, Cathay, c. 1950. This attractive view of Langton Street, looking towards St Mary Redcliffe, shows one of several streets of small, late-Georgian terraces developed along the north bank of the New Cut following completion of the Floating Harbour in 1809. In the late 1950s and early 1960s they were cleared to make way for several large blocks of council flats.

Greenbank Avenue, Lower Easton, mid-1950s. These terraced houses built in about 1898 have a single-storey bay window which shares a roof with the neighbouring bay. The narrow frontages of small Victorian terraces like this were criticised in the 1919 Tudor Walters Report, which set the standards for subsequent council house design and much suburban development – private and public alike – over the next few decades, aiming to provide a more spacious environment in place of the congestion and monotony of older developments like this.

The rear view of the houses seen from the front, above, in Greenbank Avenue, mid-1950s. Rear extensions containing a back kitchen were a feature of most working-class terraced houses built in the second half of the nineteenth century; Many consisted of two storeys – the upper room serving as a small third bedroom – but this row has only single-storey extensions containing a scullery nearest the house; next is the WC with its unmistakable saw-tooth door (providing ventilation),and the coal shed at the back.

Hallway of 65 Elmdale Road, Bedminster, September 1956. Built in 1901, this house has a narrow hall with an inner front door embellished with ruby, blue and etched glass and a decorative arch supporting the bedroom wall above. The stairs are on the right beyond the door to the front parlour while the back room – sometimes called the kitchen – contains a fitted dresser. The back kitchen still has the original kitchen range but these had generally fallen out of use in Bristol by the 1930s with the adoption of gas cookers, one of which can be clearly seen on the left.

Glendare Street, Barton Hill before redevelopment, 11 November 1953. Barton Hill grew after the opening of the Feeder Canal and the Great Western Cotton Factory in 1838. By 1952 it was one of the most densely populated areas in the city – consisting mainly of nineteenth-century terraced houses with negligible public or private open space. The houses on the left were demolished to make way for Glendare House, an eleven-storey block of flats constructed in 1958 and demolished in 1995 because of problems with its construction. The low hill beyond the end of the street was the 'Brillos', a chemical waste tip.

Backs of old houses in Cathay, Redcliff, c. 1950. These houses were demolished shortly afterwards to make way for a council development of blocks of flats built in the 1950s. The cutting in the foreground is the Bristol Harbour line from Temple Meads to the docks, which passed into a tunnel beneath Pump Lane. The railway line closed in 1964 but the embankment remains, and Pump Lane, immediately east of St Mary Redcliffe, retains its granite sets. The steep slope of Totterdown is visible to the left of St Luke's church, while the white smoke below the hill probably belongs to a steam train on its way to the south-west.

King Street looking across Whitehouse Street to Hillgrove Street, Bedminster, *c.* 1950. Before the war the area between York Road and the main railway line to the south-west was a densely packed area of streets of small terraced houses and shops. There were three public houses alone on Whitehouse Street: the Masons Arms, the Angel and the Barley Mow. Several bombs fell here during the blitz, including a land mine which completely destroyed the Chequers public house; the Masons Arms was also destroyed in a bomb raid. Cleared after the war, the area became the site of the Bedminster Trading Estate, with the first factories in business by 1952.

The view across King Street to Parker Brothers Tannery in Whitehouse Street, Bedminster, *c.* 1950. The Angel public house opposite the tannery on the corner of Sargent Street had closed by the mid-1950s.

Old Quarry Road, Penpole Housing Estate, 1950s. The 150 dwellings on this estate were built by the Ministry of Munitions towards the end of the First World War to house munitions workers, and were purchased soon afterwards by the City Council. Consisting mainly of blocks of four and six, with generous sized gardens, the houses were arranged on three new roads near Avonmouth: Kings Weston Avenue, Old Quarry Road and The Bean Acre.

The living room of a house in Old Quarry Road, 1950s. While the external design and layout of the council estates after 1919 represented a complete break with the past, the internal arrangements relied upon proven Victorian technology: gas lighting and coal-fired cooking; the joinery details, including the fitted dresser beside the range and the picture rail, are also traditional in design. The room preserves something of the flavour of a Victorian parlour in this 1950s view, even though it has acquired electric lighting and a radio.

Scullery, Old Quarry Road, 1950s. This scene, reminiscent of a seventeenth-century Dutch painting, shows the basic facilities of a 1920s council house scullery: a single cold tap over a white ceramic sink, a wooden drain board and, on the right, a coal-fired washing copper used to boil clothes and usually lit early on Monday mornings. The staggered brickwork of the flue from the copper can be seen against the wall. Tide washing powder was introduced by Proctor & Gamble in 1950.

Melton Crescent, Horfield, *c.* 1930. A turning off Wordsworth Road developed between 1926 and 1929, Melton Crescent contains a mixture of house types including semi-detached houses with and without gables, and blocks of four houses. Wordsworth Road runs across the picture, while the unfinished road in the foreground is Bonnington Walk. The mix of house types created a more spacious and carefully planned environment than the rows of Victorian terraces, but the scheme was repeated with little variation over too large an area: each turning off Wordsworth Road was treated the same way, with a semi-detached gabled house placed on the corner at an angle. Unfortunately, the repetition created its own monotony, which was precisely the criticism levelled at council estates like this after the war.

Duckmoor Road, Ashton, 11 July 1968. The Duckmore Road estate was developed by the Council in 1926. This photograph was taken after the heavy rainfall on the night of Wednesday 10 July 1968 when more than 4 in of rain fell on almost the whole of Bristol, flooding much of Ashton and Bedminster. Water rose to bedroom level at Brixham Road, Clinton Road and Marksbury Road, while Winterstoke Road was blocked for a quarter of a mile by water.

The Prince of Wales visiting new houses in Dings Walk, 6 November 1934. The Prince of Wales was particularly concerned with the problems of slum dwellers nationwide, and came to see these new homes built to replace nearby slums. The Royal Daimler carries the standard of the Prince of Wales.

No. 118 Fishponds Road, Eastville, 1956. The Lord Mayor and Lady Mayoress, Mr and Mrs Chamberlain, attract a crowd of curious onlookers as they inspect a Bristol Corporation housing improvement demonstration. Home improvement grants were made available for modernising older property to bring them up to accepted standards. This particular property had been purchased by the Council in 1956.

New private houses in Forest Road, Fishponds, *c.* 1925. About 60 per cent of the houses built in Bristol between the war were built by private developers.

The Bow dining set from the catalogue of Lenthall Brothers, furniture makers and upholsterers, Bedminster, *c.* 1935. Lenthall's produced a range of bedroom, dining room and living room suites in traditional style – evoking the Tudor period to complement the retrospective designs of the typical 1930s private house – or in the modern style. The Bow dining set, which was priced at 15 gns, curiously combines the two: the sideboard is in the modern style with rounded ends, while the dining table and chairs borrow motifs from the sixteenth and seventeenth century. Lenthalls named most of their range after local places: the catalogue includes Redcliffe, Backwell and Barton dining room suites, a Clevedon settee and easy chairs, and Wrington and Ashton bedroom suites.

A four-bedroom detached residence in Falcondale Road, designed by James and Meredith and illustrated in the 1936 brochure of Stone & Co., builders of Redland, Bristol. Falcondale Road was developed as part of the Henbury Hill Estate in the mid-1930s by Stone & Co., whose slogan was 'Architectural details faithfully interpreted'. The estate included houses ranging from semi-detached dwellings in Westover Close costing £750 to large detached houses built to 'suit purchasers' requirements' in Northover Road overlooking Henbury Golf Course: these started at £1,500. Double-fronted detached houses costing £995 were built on Passage Road, while slightly smaller houses in Falcondale Road were £975. The exterior design was a mixture of traditional motifs: the steeply pitched roof, tall chimney-stacks, leaded lights and hanging tiles in the double-storey bay window. Inside the emphasis was placed on convenience for the housewife, with an 'easiwork' kitchen and stairs built in the 'modern dust proof style'.

The 'Ashton' tiled fireplace, from the catalogue of the Metal Agencies Company, Winterstoke Road, 1954. This lounge fireplace with mottled eggshell tiles was typical of the 1930s to 1950s. With unconscious irony the MAC – celebrating their centenary year in 1954 – described this as a modern design with a semi-Tudor arch! In the 1960s tiled fireplaces rapidly fell from favour and rough stonework – or 'Cotswold stone' – fireplaces became popular; however, many new houses built after about 1960 were equipped with full central heating and had no fireplace: the centuries-old association between hearth and home had been broken.

Mother with twin pram, *c.* 1947. The photographs on these two pages are believed to have been taken by the Fry's official photographer for the City Council, probably for publicity purposes, to show the 'brave new world' of life on a city council estate in the immediate post-war years. The identity of the family and the precise location are unknown, but the setting may be Lawrence Weston, Henbury, or Southmead, where the building of council homes was proceeding at a dramatic rate at this time.

The fireplace forms the focal point of this council house living room and reading is the main recreation in about 1947, just a few years before the universal spread of television and the decline of open fires following the Clean Air Act of 1956. The furnishings appear fairly spartan, perhaps because the family have just moved in; father sits in a Lloyd Loom chair.

Chat over the garden fence, *c*. 1947. Council houses were generally provided with good sized gardens and the Council were keen that tenants should take up gardening and grow vegetables. The straight concrete path running down the centre was a common feature of the council house back garden and conveniently followed the route of the washing line.

A happy scene at tea-time: mother cuts the loaf of bread, which may have been rationed at the time, while father pours the tea. The wireless set presides over the scene. By 1947 BBC radio entertainment consisted of the Home Service, the Light Programme, a combination of light music, comedy and light drama, introduced in 1945 and the Third Programme, which followed in 1946. They provided the core of the BBC's radio network until 1967.

Aerial view of Lawrence Weston, looking south over the junction of Long Cross and Kings Weston Road, 1950s. Consisting of over 600 acres of farmland, this was one of several new housing estates developed shortly after the war, and within a decade had been transformed by the building of several thousand houses and blocks of flats. Shops, schools, churches and a library were provided to create a self-contained community, following the neighbourhood unit principle adopted by the City Council after the war. The City Council's 1952 Development Plan envisaged a population density of nineteen people per acre in Lawrence Weston – less than half the average of Bristol's older industrial suburbs.

Hungerford Road, Stockwood Estate, late 1950s. 'Easyform' two-storey flats of concrete, cast on site, were built in 1957 on the Stockwood Estate, 824 acres of agricultural land developed from the mid-1950s to rehouse people from condemned property in the old inner city suburbs such as St Philip's Marsh.

A woman with her daughter receiving attention from a housing officer, possibly applying for council accommodation, *c*. 1948. In 1946 the waiting list for council housing reached a peak of 26,661, and dealing with this and other aspects of the management of the council estates led to the growth after 1919 of a large administrative workforce to meet the needs of tenants and, of course, to collect their rent.

Fifteen-storey blocks in Barton Hill, late 1950s. New blocks of flats were built in Barton Hill from the mid-1950s, starting with the fifteen-storey block Barton House. The City retained some of the older properties in this 22-acre 'neighbourhood unit' in order to prevent the old community from breaking up. Visually the result was disastrous, because of the difference in scale between the old and the new housing and the arid open spaces around the tower blocks.

St Peter's House, Jacob's Wells Road, late 1950s. The windowless side wall of this block of eight-storey maisonettes, designed by the City Architect, J. Nelson Meredith, in 1952, provides a backdrop to the belisha beacon on the pedestrian crossing at the bottom of Jacob's Wells Road. The block took its name from the late nineteenth-century church which stood on this site until 1939. The entrance to White Hart Steps leading up into Clifton was incorporated in the building, and can be seen on the left.

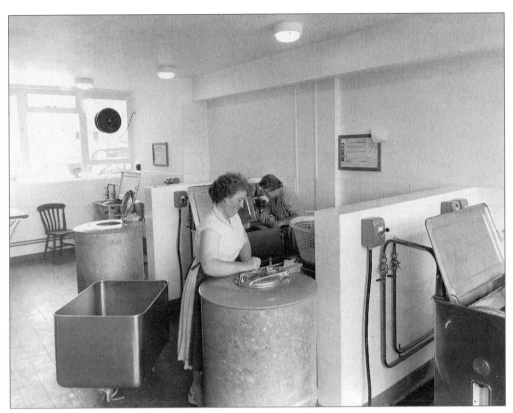

Laundry room in a council block, Redcliff, 22 July 1960. The council's post-war blocks of flats and maisonettes included a communal laundry, and this view shows the equipment that was standard for more than two decades: Electrolux washing machines with horizontal cylindrical tubs and large spin dryers. For the majority of residents who would have previously washed clothes using a gas or coal boiler followed by hand scrubbing, this was almost certainly their first encounter with an electric washing machine.

Waring House, Commercial Road, Redcliff, c. 1960. This huge L-shaped block of council maisonettes, flats and bedsits overlooking the New Cut was completed in 1960.

Norton Farmhouse, Station Road, Henbury, 1964. Many old farms lying on the outskirts of Bristol disappeared under bricks and mortar as Bristol continued its inexorable growth outwards. Norton Farm disappeared under private housing in 1964 and the old farmhouse with its large old-fashioned kitchen, dairy and cider cellar was demolished in August 1964.

Passage Road, Brentry, 1969. Passage Road contains Bristol's first pelican crossing, which opened in July 1969.

CHAPTER FIFTEEN

LEISURE & RECREATION

From the 1920s and 1930s leisure began to feature as prominently as work in the lives of Bristolians. People had more leisure time as average working hours fell from fifty-three hours a week at the beginning of the twentieth century to forty-two by the 1960s. During the 1920s one-and-a-half million wage earners were entitled to a holiday with pay; by 1938 the figure was three million; and as a result of the Holidays with Pay Act passed in that year the figure rose to eleven million. People also had more disposable income to spend on leisure pursuits: between 1913 and 1938 real wages increased by 50 per cent, while expenditure on such basics as food and rent decreased. Leisure time could be spent in a variety of ways. It was a matter of personal taste and of social class: going to the pub or a football match were predominantly working-class pursuits, while cricket and theatre-going tended to attract a middle-class audience. Many people looked to the theatre or cinema for entertainment, while others developed their leisure time in home-based activities such as gardening and other hobbies. Forms of entertainment tended to lose their local character: as cinema-goers watched American films in picture houses run by national companies, and at home families tuned in to the British Broadcasting Corporation from London, it became increasingly difficult to find a local identity to entertainment and leisure in Bristol.

In the 1920s and 1930s concerts, serious plays, pantomime and popular variety entertainment were staged at several theatres in Bristol. Classical concerts were held at the Colston Hall and the Victoria Assembly Rooms. The Prince's Theatre was visited by important touring companies and many celebrated actors with their London companies took the stage there. Plays could also be seen at the Theatre Royal in King Street – the oldest theatre in the country, established in 1766 – and the Little Theatre in Colston Street, established in 1923, which was described in Bristol's 1926 Official Guide as one of the leading repertory theatres in the country. Variety entertainment was staged at the Empire in Old Market and the Hippodrome on St Augustine's Parade; both these venues had been established when the popularity of music halls was its height, and for a time maintained their role as places of variety entertainment hosting singers, comedians such as Max Miller and dance companies. By 1920, however, the music hall was under siege from a new competitor: the cinema.

Bristol's first cinema was the Bio, opened in Counterslip Hall in 1908, and by 1920 there were about thirty-five picture houses in the city. Huge crowds flocked to them: their appeal cut across all social classes, although attendance was highest among the least well off for whom the cinema was a place of escape. Cinemas were glamorous. Their architects created palaces; for example, the Bristol architect, William Henry Watkins, designed several including the Regent in Castle Street – one of the largest and finest in the city. Designed in 1926–7, the Regent's interior of red, purple and gold was an opulent fantasy world of florid plasterwork surmounted by an impressive dome. Music was the essential accompaniment to the silent movie. The largest cinemas, such as the Regent, had space for orchestras; soloists were engaged to sing – their repertoire complementing the mood of the film – while many cinemas had organs capable of producing thunderous sound effects. The coming of the 'talkies' came as something of a surprise at first, but they soon ousted the silent film – and the orchestras and soloists. The first showing of a film with sound was Al Jolson's *Singing Fool*, screened at the King's in Old Market. Other cinemas rapidly wired their auditoriums for sound, and by mid-1931 all Bristol's cinemas had been converted. The cinema decimated its competitors. Variety was the chief victim: the Bedminster Hippodrome, opened in 1911, had lasted for only four years as a music hall before being converted to a cinema; the Empire became a cinema in 1931 and the Bristol Hippodrome in 1933.

Twelve new cinemas opened in the 1930s, including the Embassy on Queens Road – Bristol's largest with 2,100 seats – which opened in 1933, and the Odeon, a striking example of modern architecture, opened by Oscar Deutsch in 1938 on the site of the Fry's offices on the corner of Union Street and Nelson Street (see page 188). By 1939 there were some forty cinemas in Bristol distributed widely across the city, from the Savoy in Shirehampton to the Gaiety in Knowle. No other form of entertainment penetrated the suburbs so effectively, and in new areas of housing where amenities were few, cinemas provided a welcome diversion.

Sport occupied many people's leisure time. Some of the large companies such as Imperial Tobacco organised their own football and cricket leagues, and there were many other opportunities for taking part in a wide range of sports including rugby, swimming, golf, cycling, skittles, bowls and billiards. Bristolians could watch association football at Ashton Gate or Eastville, rugby at the Horfield Memorial Ground or county cricket at Horfield. Professional cricket and football attracted large crowds. In 1930, 17,000 people watched Gloucestershire's tie with the Australians in 1930 and in the 1934/5 football season over 47,000 Bristol City supporters (including 5,000 who charged the gates and got in free) saw their team beat Portsmouth 2–0 in a cup fixture. Football pools were a 1930s' creation and widened the appeal of football. They were big business, too: in 1938 £40 million was spent on the pools. Bets were also placed on dogs: greyhound racing took place at Eastville and Knowle stadiums.

There were many other things that people could do for amusement, such as going to the Downs, Bristol Zoo, or the Blaise Castle Estate, which after 1926 was freely open to the public; there was fishing at Blagdon and a choice of trips by motor bus or charabanc to West Country beauty spots such as Cheddar Gorge or Tintern Abbey. In the summer months there were excursions on Campbell's pleasure steamers from the Hotwells landing stage to Ilfracombe, Clevedon, Weston-super-Mare, Lynton or South Wales. There were restaurants, cafes, public houses, museums to visit – or the option of staying at home.

The 1920s and 1930s saw an increase in the importance of home-based leisure activities. Life on suburban estates away from the distractions of city centre life encouraged the development of the home as a centre of private relaxation. Gardening, reading – thrillers and detective stories were all the rage in the 1930s – stamp collecting, knitting and listening to the wireless set were individual forms of relaxation shared by thousands and sustained by commercial interests. The radio spread rapidly from the late 1920s as the mains-powered radio was perfected and householders received electricity: by 1939 nine in ten homes in Britain owned a wireless set. On 3 September 1939 many people in Bristol, as elsewhere, tuned in to their radios to hear the Prime Minister, Neville Chamberlain, announce that a state of war existed between Great Britain and Germany, and over the next six years followed the course of the war by radio news broadcasts.

The war inevitably disrupted leisure and entertainment. The first major raid on Bristol, on the night of 24 November 1940, saw the destruction of the Prince's Theatre and the Regent cinema in Castle Street; five other cinemas went in the blitz and several others were badly damaged. The post-war period saw changes in the pattern of leisure in the city. The remaining theatres survived and flourished: the Bristol Old Vic Company was established in February 1946, and in October that year Sir Laurence Olivier opened the Old Vic Theatre School. The Colston Hall, damaged by fire after the war, was completely refurbished and continued to offer classical concerts and other forms of entertainment, but the cinemas suffered a catastrophic and sudden decline. The attraction of alternative family and home-based activities were the root cause: in particular there was the lure of television which by 1963 was found in 82 per cent of British homes. Increasing car ownership was another factor, extending people's mobility and widening the choice of things to do. And so the cinemas closed to become bingo halls, supermarkets or freezer centres, and by the mid-1960s only a few survived. Just one cinema began showing pictures in this decade – as part of the New Bristol Entertainment Centre opened in Frogmore Street in 1966 – and it started life with a visit from the Lord Mayor and a showing of *Dr Zhivago*.

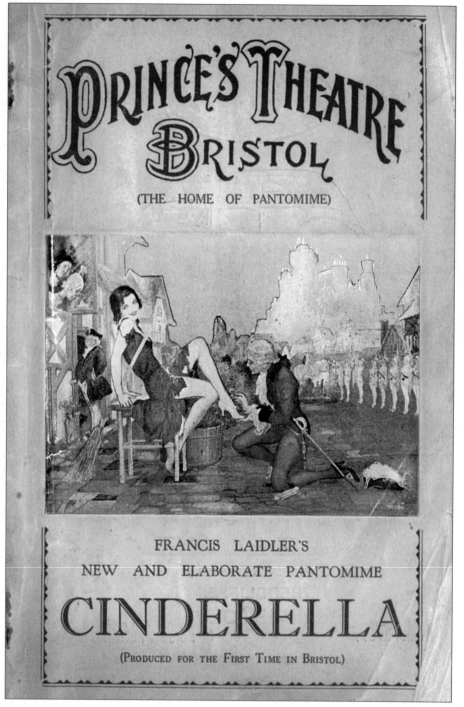

PRINCE'S THEATRE
BRISTOL
(THE HOME OF PANTOMIME)

FRANCIS LAIDLER'S
NEW AND ELABORATE PANTOMIME

CINDERELLA
(PRODUCED FOR THE FIRST TIME IN BRISTOL)

Theatre programme for *Cinderella*, produced by Francis Laidler at the Prince's Theatre, Park Row, commencing 25 December 1937. Pantomine had been a regular feature of the theatre from its opening in 1867. This production starred Phyllis Godden as Prince Charming, Joan Cole as Cinderella with Jack Hayes and Victor King as the Ugly Sisters. The production included dance sequences by the John Tiller Girls and the Turner Twins.

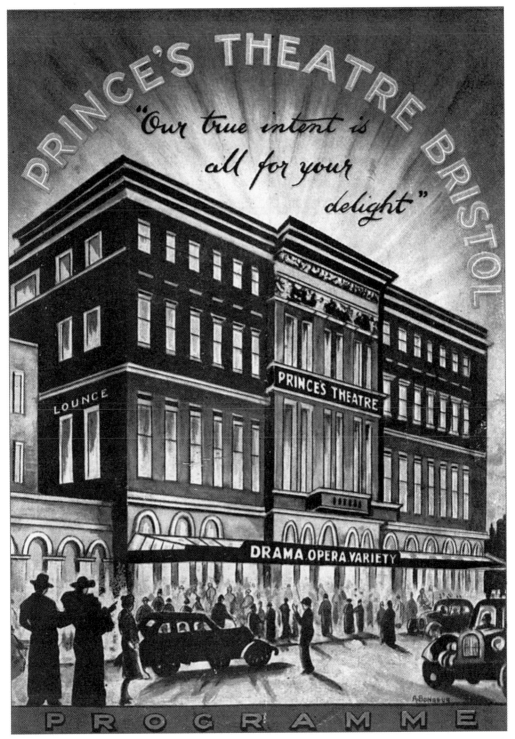

Theatre programme for Verdi's *La Traviata*, performed by the Carl Rosa Opera Company at the Prince's Theatre from 22 April 1940. Seven months later the life of the Theatre Royal came to an abrupt end in the blitz on the night of 24 November 1940.

Amateur dramatics at Bishopston Parish Hall, *The Man in the Bowler Hat*, 20 March 1929. Margaret Sherrell, who is seated second from the left, lived at Downend Park Farm, Horfield.

Queens Picture House, Peter Street, *c.* 1930. This 500-seat cinema was Bristol's first purpose-built cinema and opened in 1910. In 1933 it closed and was replaced by the News Theatre, which had a modern front in glass and chrome; it showed newsreel and cartoon programmes and survived until 1956.

Regent cinema, Castle Street, July 1936. This cinema, with seating for 2,014 people, was built for the Provincial Cinematographic Theatres Ltd and opened in July 1928. It was designed by the Bristol architect W.H. Watkins, who designed several cinemas in Bristol between 1910 and the 1930s. The poster advertises Michael Redgrave with Jean Kent and John Greenwood in the *The Man Within* in Technicolor from Monday 7 July, and also exclusive film of the finalists entering the Rose Queen contest. One of the largest and finest cinemas in Bristol, it had a short life – being a victim of the blitz of 24 November 1940.

The Clifton Suspension Bridge illuminated for the 1951 Festival of Britain. The tradition of illuminating the bridge dates to the opening on 8 December 1864, when arc lights were used.

Ashton Court, 1964. Comprising 850 acres of parkland, Ashton Court was purchased from the Smyth estate in 1959 although the grounds had been open to the public on many occasions for use by the Boy Scouts and the staging of the Bristol Pageant in 1924.

Bristol Zoo, 1950s. Founded in 1835, Bristol Zoo is the fifth oldest in the world. In 1927, after a period of decline, when it was largely used as a fair and venue for fêtes, the zoo developed its zoological and horticultural collections in line with its original objectives. A new aquarium, sea lion pool, new monkey house and polar bear enclosure were built and attendances rose. This view along the Terrace looking towards the aquarium shows the lion house, one of the original buildings, which was replaced in about 1962.

Bristol Zoo, 1950s. The elephant Rosie was a former circus animal acquired by the zoo in 1938; she was very tame and gave rides on her howdah to thousands of children every year. She is seen here in the company of Tom Bartlett, the elephant keeper. Rosie died in 1961.

Entrance to the Blaise Castle Estate, Henbury Road, *c.* 1955. The estate had been in the hands of the Harford family since 1789 but in 1926 they sold it to the City Council which opened it to the public. The walks through the dramatic scenery of the 191 acres of parkland soon made a popular day out for Bristolians. The entrance seen here is just beyond Henbury post office, on the left, which was relocated to Station Road at the end of November 1997. This narrow part of Henbury Road became one way in 1967.

The paddling pool, Blaise Castle Estate, 1956.

Blaise Castle House, *c*. 1950. Following use of the house by the armed forces during the war, a café was opened, and then in 1949 it became a museum of West of England Folk Life run by the City Council.

Blaise Mansion café, *c*. 1947. This café opened in Blaise Castle House after the war, and was situated in the former picture gallery of the house designed by Charles Cockerell and built in about 1832–3. Run by Civic Catering, the room became a popular venue for wedding receptions in the 1950s and early 1960s. The waitress is Eileen Irwin née Croker, who died aged twenty-seven.

Eastville United Methodist Football Team, 1927. Eastville UM were champions of Wesleyan and Free Church League in 1927.

Fry's works football team, photographed at Somerdale, 1939.

CHAPTER SIXTEEN

LOCAL GOVERNMENT & SERVICES

L ocal government influence on the running of the city was at its greatest in the mid-twentieth century. From the 1830s, starting with such humble duties as street lighting and establishing a police force, the role of local government widened in the second half of the nineteenth century to include responsibility for public health, parks, cemeteries, libraries and, after 1902, education. The 1919 Housing Act placed the responsibility for housing in the hands of the City, and additional legislation in the 1930s and 1940s further widened the City's authority in the field of health and town planning. The City Council was also a major landowner in Bristol: it managed the largest municipally owned port in the country, and from 1930 was also responsible for the airport.

During this period Bristol was a City and County Borough. In the 1920s the government of Bristol consisted of a Lord Mayor, twenty-three aldermen elected by their fellow-councillors for six years, and sixty-nine councillors representing the various wards of the city elected by the voters of Bristol for three years. The administration of the city was delegated to specialist committees made up of councillors. It was in committees that the important decisions affecting the future of the city were made. There was much prestige and interest, therefore, attached to being a local councillor, although the room for independent initiative was less than it had been in the nineteenth century. The Council was predominantly an instrument of national policy, with roughly 40 per cent of its income derived from government grants. Many of the far-reaching schemes for the building of new council estates and improved health and educational services were born of national legislation: while the Council's role widened in this period, therefore, the initiative lay firmly with central government, and the limitations of the Council's freedom of movement were often only too apparent, as in 1947, when it found its ambitious plans for the rebuilding of the city curtailed by central government; the indignation and dismay of local councillors was considerable but they were powerless.

Most Bristolians saw little of this; the visible side of local government was largely ceremonial. The Council had abolished several ceremonial positions in the late nineteenth century to save money but formal civic occasions were still accompanied by colourful and archaic pageantry. The formal dress of the officials harked back to the eighteenth century, but many of the traditions themselves had their roots in the founding of the Council in 1373. The swearing in of a new Lord Mayor was one such formal occasion when police could be seen holding up traffic at the bottom of Park Street: for a few moments twentieth-century Bristol was held at bay while medieval officialdom – the Lord Mayor, the Sheriff, aldermen and others, led by the City Sword Bearer carrying an eighteenth-century sword – crossed from the Council House to St Mark's, the Lord Mayor's chapel, for a service. The Lord Mayor's chapel is unique in being the only municipally owned church in the country. The opening of the Bristol Assizes was also marked by a formal occasion involving the Lord Mayor, the city's chief magistrate, who joined the visiting judges for a service in the Lord Mayor's chapel. The journey across the centre to the Guildhall where the court was located was an impressive sight: the company travelled in the Lord Mayor's state coach with an escort of mounted police carrying swords; City trumpeters heralded their arrival at the chapel and the Guildhall. This colourful ritual survived until the abolition of the Assize courts in 1971.

The mid-twentieth century saw considerable expansion in the City Council. In 1935 the wards of the city were increased to twenty-three represented by sixty-nine councillors; the following year the number of wards was increased again to twenty-eight and the Council enlarged to 112 members. Following the extension of the vote to women in 1918 and 1928, women entered local politics, and by 1930 there were several women serving on Council committees. Mrs L.M. Pheysey was elected the first woman councillor in 1920 and first woman alderman in 1932; and in 1963 Florence Brown became the first female Lord Mayor. The management and administration of the new areas of responsibility and the expansion of others resulted in a large increase in the City Council workforce. New departments and new posts were established. After 1930 a post of Commandant was created to run the airport, in 1938 the Council appointed its first City Architect and a Planning Department (albeit under the City Engineer) was created in 1947. Before the war the various departments were based in various buildings in the city, while the formal business was conducted in the Council House in Corn Street. By the early twentieth century this was regarded as unworthy of so large and wealthy a community, and in 1919 the Council purchased property on College Green for new municipal buildings. Work was slow to start and it was not until 1935 that the foundation stone was laid, then progress on the building was halted by the war – and it was not opened formally until 1956. Occupying a commanding site on a re-landscaped College Green, the new Council House was the physical manifestation of the central role of twentieth-century local government in the running of the city. By the time of its completion it was not large enough to accommodate the growing workforce, and in 1957 Cabot House was built behind the Council House on Deanery Road for the City Engineer's Department.

The Local Government Act of 1929 brought about major changes in local government. The Board of Guardians established in 1834, which had administered the workhouse system of relief, was abolished and its responsibilities transferred to the Council, which found itself responsible for hospitals, care of the poor and the mentally sick. The Council was now responsible for virtually all the welfare of the city, although charitable and voluntary bodies still continued to support several schools and hospitals with the aid of government grants. There were also several old-established charities in the City responsible for some twenty almshouses which provided several hundred places for elderly persons. Following the 1929 Act Southmead Hospital, formerly administered by the Board of Guardians, was taken over and a Bristol Hospitals Council formed to co-ordinate the work of the voluntary and municipal hospitals in the city. In 1947 the National Health Service was established by the post-war Labour Government to create a completely free and universal health service, and this brought all hospitals under the control of the Ministry of Health. Major hospital extensions in the vicinity of the Bristol Royal Infirmary and on St Michaels Hill – an area which the City Council 'zoned' for hospital use after the war – were built from the late 1950s, including the BRI hospital chimney, one of the city's major landmarks (albeit not a particularly attractive one), which was erected in 1965. The City Council, nevertheless, continued to provide a wide range of health services including the provision of a home nursing service, clinics and health centres, day nurseries and the ambulance service.

The City Council had been responsible for education at both primary and secondary level since 1902, although Bristol was remarkable for the number of its independent schools – some of which were of ancient foundation, such as Queen Elizabeth's Hospital, Bristol Grammar School and Red Maids' School. Developments in local authority-administered schools in the 1920s and 1930s saw a widening of the curriculum, a reduction in class sizes and an improvement in the quality of teachers. In 1919 the City Council's Education Committee established three Bristol Central Schools for east, north and south Bristol. They were intended to fill the gap between the elementary schools and the secondary schools: the latter were subsequently renamed grammar schools and the City provided three of these – Fairfield, Merrywood and St George. The Education Act of 1944 required the City to assess its requirements for education. The rise in the birth rate during the war years, the movement of population to new housing estates and the replacing of the 7,000 school places lost during the war, together with the raising of the school leaving age to fifteen in 1947, resulted in a considerable pressure on school accommodation, and the building of new schools was an important priority for the Council in the immediate post-war years: between 1945 and 1951, fourteen new schools were built. In 1954 the first comprehensive schools were opened at Lockleaze and Hengrove; by 1973 sixty-eight primary schools and twenty-three secondary schools had been built since 1946.

The Bristol Constabulary dates from 1836, and in the second half of the nineteenth century had assumed a wide range of responsibilities including detective investigation, river policing, fire fighting and the provision of an ambulance service. Developments after the First World War took account of changes in society, the introduction of new technology and the huge rise of motor traffic. In 1920 the only motor car in the police force was the Chief Constable's car, but following the passing of the Road Traffic Act in 1930 motor patrols were introduced. The parking of cars in the city centre had become a problem by the 1930s: in 1936, to meet the complaints of motorists of the inadequacy of car parking facilities in the city, the Council issued a pamphlet: 'Where to Park Your Car in the Centre of Bristol'. But the responsibility for policing the arrangements fell to the police, and the problem only worsened in the post-war years as the number of cars increased. In 1961 Bristol was the first city outside London to introduce parking meters, and the same year twenty-five traffic wardens were appointed to ensure that motorists used them – many had threatened not to – and in 1967 they were joined by the first female traffic wardens or 'meter maids'. Police communications improved after 1932 with the introduction of police telephone pillars, which could be used both by the police and the public. They remained a familiar sight in the city until 1968 when personal radios were introduced as part of the unit beat system, where constables patrolled on foot with the backing of a panda car – so called because of their distinctive appearance. The 999 emergency telephone service was another innovation of this period, being introduced in 1946. The Bridewell Street headquarters were rebuilt in 1928 and officially opened in 1930, while new police stations were established at Knowle, Bishopsworth and Lockleaze. Women police first appeared during the First World War and by 1918 there were eighteen on patrol in Bristol. At first they were unpopular with their male counterparts, and were required to patrol in pairs with two men following a few yards behind; and although they formed their own separate division in 1920 it was not until 1931 that women were sworn in as constables.

The City Council provided many other services in the city including libraries, museums, the Colston Hall and the Little Theatre. The care of the streets lay with the Council: the 1930s saw many streets resurfaced with tarmacadam – replacing the granite sets used in the nineteenth century; the City Council also ensured that roads were swept and maintained thousands of street lights. Gas street lamps declined over this period. Electric lamps had first been introduced in 1893 and had been extended to most of the City's principal streets in the Edwardian decade. By about 1930 the use of electric lamps was extended to new roads across the city; gas lighting, meanwhile, remained common in the older nineteenth-century suburbs until the 1950s, but was confined to just a few locations by 1969. The City also emptied the dustbins, carried out food inspections, and its Weights and Measures Department verified and stamped weights and measures and carried out spot checks on the delivery of coal, bread and other articles. The creation of the National Health Service and the nationalisation of the electricity industry by the post-war Labour government removed two important functions from local authority control, but in other fields, such as planning, the role of local government continued to expand, ensuring that the City Council continued to be a major force in shaping the modern city.

The Council House, College Green, *c.* 1960. Over twenty years passed between the laying of the foundation stone of the new Council House, designed by E. Vincent Harris, and its formal opening by Queen Elizabeth II in 1956. This low-angle shot emphasises the long curve of the building and the barren and windswept open space created in front of it when the trees on the Green were cut down between 1950 and 1951. The replica high cross which had stood on the Green since 1850 was also removed.

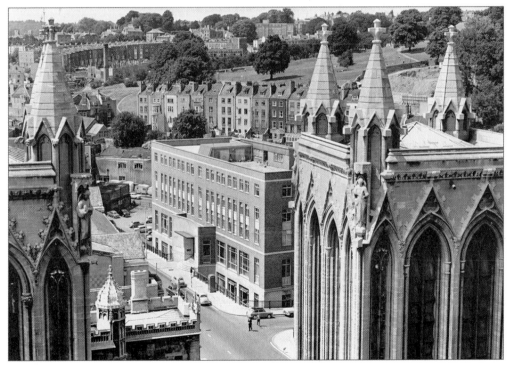

Cabot House, Deanery Road, from the roof of the Cathedral, late 1950s. This block of Council offices was designed by the City Architect, A.H. Clark, and built in 1957.

The Lord Mayor accompanied by HM Judges and the Sheriff pass St Augustine's Parade, on their way to the Guildhall for the opening of the Bristol Assizes following a service in the Lord Mayor's chapel, *c.* 1935. They are travelling in the Lord Mayor's coach, which dated from the mid-nineteenth century and was modified in about 1890, and have an escort of mounted police carrying swords. The Bristol Assizes and Quarter Sessions were abolished by the Courts Act of 1971, and the Assizes were last held in Bristol on 3 October 1971.

Police stop traffic in Park Street as the Lady Lord Mayor, Alderman Florence Mills Brown, takes her successor, Kenelm Antony Philip Dalby, to a service in the Lord Mayor's chapel, 1964. The procession from the Council House includes the Sheriff (seen in front of the bus) and is led by the City Sword Bearer, J.L. Purchase.

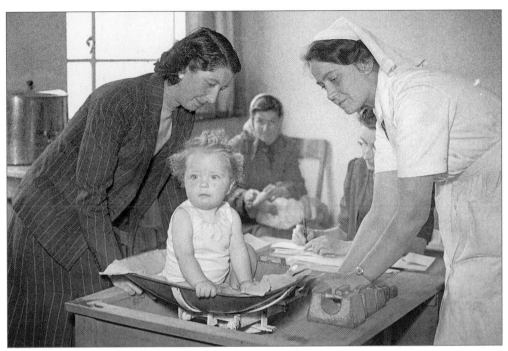

Health Department clinics, 1940s. A health visitor at a City Council Infant Welfare Centre weighs a baby to check for normal growth.

St Raphael's Almshouses, Cumberland Road, 1930s. These almshouses were adjacent to St Raphael's church, founded as a seamen's mission and consecrated in 1859. The church and almshouses were designed by Henry Woodyer. The almshouses consisted of a simple row with a large tiled roof, half-timbered dormers and a secluded wooden cloister walk. They were damaged during the war and demolished in October 1970.

Red Maids' Founder's Day, November 1959. Red Maids' School was founded in 1634 by John Witson (1557 or 1558–1629), a wealthy Bristol merchant who stipulated in his will that the girls should be clothed in red cloth. The school moved from premises in Denmark Street to Westbury-on-Trym in 1911.

Upper Horfield School, Sheridan Road, Horfield, May 1937. Class 5 is decorated with flags to mark the Coronation of George VI. In this elementary school, which opened in 1929, the children sit behind iron-framed desks with seats and top cut from solid oak.

Ashton Vale Primary School, Avebury Road, Ashton Vale, 8 March 1951. Opened in 1949 to cater for the large number of infants on the new Ashton Vale estate, this primary school was typical of those built after the war by the Education Committee. The informal arrangement of tables and chairs was a far cry from the serried ranks of desks in the older elementary schools. 'All of them', wrote the *Evening World* in 1956, 'are a small world of plastic, plate glass and pastel shades.'

Hengrove Comprehensive School, Petherton Gardens, Hengrove, *c*. 1954. This was one of the first two comprehensive schools in the city, although at first they were called 'mixed' schools to distinguish them from secondary modern and grammar schools. Plans by the Labour group on the Council to expand comprehensive education and phase out the local authority grammar schools evolved around this time and were the subject of much debate.

The Bristol Constabulary Band leads the annual church parade through the city centre to Bristol Cathedral for a commemorative service in memory of the forty-one officers killed in action in the First World War, c. 1936. The band, which had existed in the 1880s, was revived in 1929 and lasted until the outbreak of war in 1939.

Detectives on church parade, the city centre, c. 1936. The detective branch of the police originated in 1880 and became the Criminal Investigation Unit in 1920.

Union Street, *c.* 1950. Constable A67 from the Bridewell gives road directions to the driver of a Morris 8 in a desolate post-war city landscape. Relations between the police and motorists have not always been as cordial as this.

Leyland Braidwood fire engine outside the Bridewell fire station, 1930s. The crew were seated on either side of a box containing the hose and other equipment. This gave no protection from the weather and there was the danger that men could be thrown off when cornering at speed. The new Fire Brigade premises, seen here, were completed in 1930, and in 1935 the strength of the Brigade stood at eighty-five men.

The Central Library, Deanery Road, *c.* 1930. The library was designed by Charles Holden and opened in June 1906. Holden, who went on to design many 1930s London underground stations, adopted a neo-Tudor style for the building. In the 1920s it was the controlling centre for eleven branch libraries in the city and it adopted the open access system in August 1924. The Folk House educational centre, to the right of the library, was bombed in the war. In this pre-war view tramlines are visible in the road.

An extension to the Central Library was proposed as early as 1952 but work did not begin on the building until March 1966; it was opened in July 1967.

Art Gallery, Queens Road, 1950s. The Art Gallery, adjoining the museum, was built by Sir William Henry Wills, later Lord Winterstoke, and was presented by him to the City in 1905; it was designed by Frank W. Wills. In 1928 it was extended by the addition of another wing, also funded by the Wills family. The art nouveau electroliers were made by Thursfield & Co., Birmingham, and the military colours from the Gloucestershire Regiment were presented to the City after the First World War, and remained on display until about 1990.

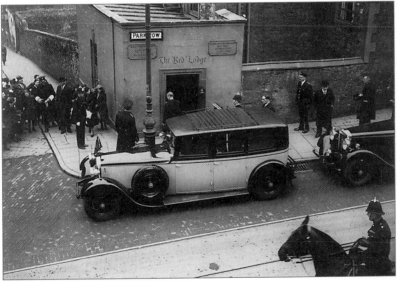

The Prince of Wales enters the Red Lodge, 6 November 1934. Having spent the morning visiting slum areas and new council housing (see page 241), the Prince of Wales was entertained to lunch by the Lord Mayor at the Red Lodge. This large town house of about 1590 with its well-preserved interior was donated to the City Council by the Bristol Savages, a men-only society of artists, in 1920; public access, however, remained limited until after the war. The Georgian House Museum in Great George Street was opened in 1939.

Bread delivery van, 1940s. A weights and measures inspector checks the weight of a loaf of bread during delivery by a roundsman, using a special balance.

Lulsgate Airport, *c.* 1965. The City Council established an airport committee in 1929 and opened Whitchurch Airport in May 1930; it was then only the third civil airport in the country. Traffic increased steadily after the war and it became clear that Whitchurch could not accommodate the anticipated expansion. Lulsgate Airport, built by the Air Ministry in 1942, was purchased by the Corporation and opened on 1 May 1958. Most of the early services from Lulsgate were operated by Cambrian Airways and Aer Lingus. Two Vickers Viscounts operated by Cambrian Airways on scheduled domestic services are seen in this view.

CHAPTER SEVENTEEN

BRISTOL BLITZED

The Second World War involved the entire nation. For the first time war with another state brought the civilian population into direct contact with the enemy on the Home Front, and people found themselves participating in the defence of their city. Bristol's civil defence involved the creation of volunteer forces of air raid wardens, street fire guards and, in case of a land invasion by the Germans, local platoons of an auxiliary force – at first known as the Local Defence Volunteers; it soon became better known as the Home Guard. Voluntary medical services such as St John's Ambulance Brigade and the British Red Cross Society also played a major role in attending to the wounded. Civilians, therefore, found themselves working alongside the armed forces, the police and full-time fire brigade in the defence of the city. But everyone in Bristol – as in other large cities – was a target as the Germans attempted to destroy civilian morale by night-time bombing of English cities during the bleak winter of 1940/1.

The announcement by the Prime Minister, Neville Chamberlain, on 3 September 1939 that a state of war existed between Britain and Germany at first made little difference to most Bristolians. Street lighting was extinguished and motor cars forbidden to use their headlamps, which led to an increase in road accidents and of people falling into the docks, but there was no immediate German attack. This was the period of the 'Phoney War'. Hitler had been taken unawares by his own success and had made no preparations for the invasion of England. Throughout the ensuing months the strengthening of air defences which had begun in 1937 continued: anti-aircraft guns, searchlights and barrage balloons were deployed around the city. The fear of a gas attack had resulted in the general issue of gas masks in late 1938; they had to be carried at all times and drills on their use were regularly carried out. Surface air-raid shelters were built and Anderson shelters – named after Sir John Anderson, the Home Secretary – were issued free to those with an income below £250 a year. Bristol's civil defence was co-ordinated by the ARP based in Broadmead, and the backbone of the ARP was the wardens' service, which was under the direct control of the Chief Constable.

The first air raid in the Bristol area occurred on 25 June 1940 when the Luftwaffe bombed St Phillips, St Pauls, St James and Brislington although they were actually aiming to destroy the works of the Bristol Aeroplane Company at Filton. There was little major damage although five people lost their lives. Several other relatively minor attacks occurred through the summer of 1940, but a serious attack on the aircraft factories at Filton took place on the morning of 25 September. One Heinkel bomber was brought down by anti-aircraft guns at Portishead – the first of only two enemy aircraft brought down by Bristol's anti-aircraft guns during the war. The other raiders reached Filton and within forty-five seconds had wrought major damage to the plant: ninety-one employees of the Bristol Aeroplane Company were killed and the development of the Bristol Beaufighter, a new fighter plane, was delayed.

With unsustainable losses being suffered during daylight attacks on Britain in mid-October 1940, the Luftwaffe turned to the night bombing of cities, and Bristol suffered its first major raid on 24 November, a Sunday evening. From about 7.00 pm until midnight 134 German aircraft dropped high explosive bombs and incendiaries on Bristol. Fire raged across the city, lighting up the sky and betraying the position of Bristol to enemy air crews from up to 50 miles away. Seventy-seven fire brigades were sent into the city to assist the Bristol force in fighting the fires. The next morning, shattered and dazed, Bristolians walked through the ruins of once-familiar streets filled with the acrid smell of burning, masses of broken glass and the melancholy drip of water. Only a skeleton structure of charred wood remained of the Dutch House; St Peter's Hospital, the jewel in the crown of Bristol's old timber framed buildings, was gone and the Upper Arcade between The Horsefair and St James Barton was destroyed; several medieval churches were badly damaged – St Peter's church, St Nicholas church, St Mary-le-Port church – although their towers all survived; several almshouses were also destroyed. Most of the shops in Wine Street and Castle Street were wiped out and Mary-le-Port Street was totally destroyed; there was also extensive damage in Victoria Street, Redcliff Street and Thomas Street. Clifton also suffered extensive damage: St Andrew's, the parish church, was bombed – although again the tower survived – only to be demolished in 1954. Queens Road, Park Street and Park Row saw extensive damage: the Prince's Theatre was destroyed; so too was the Museum and part of the Art Gallery. There was also damage to the University, including the Great Hall, and Lennards premises on Queens Road was reduced to a pile of rubble. Houses in Bedminster, Knowle and St George were also bombed. The official casualty list included 200 people killed, 163 seriously injured and 526 slightly hurt. The assertion in a German newspaper, however, that Bristol had been wiped out as a major industrial centre was a huge exaggeration, but the scale of the damage revealed how vulnerable the city was to air attack.

The Luftwaffe exploited the inadequacy of Bristol's air defences over the following months, with bad winter weather the city's only effective defence. The next major raid occurred just over a week later, on the night of 2 December, when 167 fires broke out across the city: the Bishop's Palace was destroyed, 156 people were killed and another 149 were seriously injured. The third large air raid took place on the evening of 6 December, and again caused damage to buildings in the centre as well as several industrial sites, including Parnall's aircraft works at Barton Hill. This raid killed 100 people and seriously injured eighty. The New Year began with a large-scale attack by 178 aircraft, which lasted nearly all night. Temple Meads railway station and the City Docks suffered much damage; the Corporation Granary on Princes Wharf was destroyed and St Augustine-the-Less was badly damaged. This was also one of the coldest nights of the year, and fire-fighters and other units had to combat the fires in biting cold and ice. Avonmouth was attacked on 16 January but worsening weather then forced a halt for a while, and the next major raid was not until 16 March. This raid, by 167 aircraft, hit parts of the centre which had previously escaped, and also caused extensive damage in the industrial suburbs of East Bristol; as a result, the casualties were higher on this night than at any time during the war: 257 were killed and 391 were injured. Another raid took place on 9 April and then the last large-scale raid took place on 11 April – the so-called Good Friday raid – when 153 German bombers attacked the city, causing extensive damage in areas close to the City Docks and also resulting in the destruction of Cheltenham Road public library and Colston Girl's School opposite.

The Prime Minister, Winston Churchill, was on his way to Bristol when the Good Friday raid took place, and had to delay his arrival until it was over. As Churchill toured the bomb-scarred city he was booed by some Bristolians who blamed the government for their predicament. Morale was at an all-time low after so much death and destruction during a bitterly cold winter. That Bristol suffered there can be no doubt; the Germans reckoned Bristol was the fourth most bombed city in England. Until September 1941 the enemy killed more civilians than combatants in England, and although morale in Bristol held out – just – many people suffered from considerable stress during the blitz.

From the spring of 1941 the Germans began to turn their attention towards Russia and the heavy raids stopped. There were a few sporadic attacks during the summer of 1941, but they were mainly small-scale affairs. In August 1942 a single bomb from a Junkers 86R flying largely undetected at high altitude fell on Broad Weir, killing forty-five people. The following year passed without a single raid and the final attack by the Luftwaffe on Bristol occurred on 14 May 1944. In over seventy raids on the city 1,250 people were killed, 3,000 were injured and 89,000 properties were destroyed or damaged, but Bristol survived, and industrial production increased through the war years. In May 1945 the people of Bristol celebrated victory and turned to the task of rebuilding the city.

ARP centre, 55 Broadmead, 1940. A rare view of the interior of the Bristol ARP Control, with maps on the wall showing the six ARP divisions into which the city was divided: these were Bedminster, Central, Clifton, Knowle, St George and Shirehampton. The ARP Controller appointed in 1939 was H.M. Webb, the City Engineer.

Gas mask drill in Bristol during the war. The Street Fire Parties, subsequently renamed the Fire Guard, were established to deal with small fires caused by incendiaries; the stirrup pump was their essential piece of equipment. Gas masks were issued in late 1938 and had to be carried at all times; this rule was relaxed by the government after 1942, however.

A dramatic picture of what could have happened if the Germans had released gas on Bristol; this, however, was only a drill.

The Lord Mayor, Alderman T.H.J. Underdown, gives the thumbs up to children being evacuated to Devon in 1941. Over 20,000 children were evacuated from Bristol, chiefly to Devon and Cornwall, from February 1941.

A dawn view of the corner of Broadmead and Union Street, with the Fire Brigade still attending to fires. After the war the building of the new shopping centre started at this end of Broadmead.

The corner of Park Street and Charlotte Street after the air raid of 24 November 1940: a scene of chaos as shocked citizens survey the damage in Park Street. On the night of the raid Park Street was described as an avenue of fire. The telephone kiosk is a K2 concrete model introduced in 1929; it was painted cream and red.

Lennards Corner, Queens Road. This well-known landmark in Queens Road was a victim of the first major raid on Bristol on the night of 24 November 1940. It was described as 'one surging wave of fire' by Eric Buston, a *Western Daily Press* photographer.

Wine Street after the air raid of 24 November 1940. Many fine and historic buildings were lost or damaged beyond repair in the centre of the city during this evening attack, including St Peter's Hospital and the Dutch House – the remains of which were pulled down completely by 6 December 1940. It has been said that the Dutch House proved difficult to demolish: this may have been because of the steelwork inserted when it was refurbished in 1908 (see *Bristol 1850–1919*, page 19), rather than charred seventeenth-century timbers.

Daylight air raid on Broad Weir, 28 August 1942. At 9.30 am a single 500 lb bomb was dropped on the city from a German aircraft flying undetected at over 20,000 ft. It struck Broad Weir near the junction of Philadelphia Street and three buses loaded with passengers were set on fire instantaneously. Many people were trapped in the blazing vehicles and the buses were soon reduced to twisted metal.

Daylight air raid on Broad Weir, 28 August 1942. Forty-five people were killed and twenty-six seriously wounded, while another thirty were slightly hurt; it was the biggest death toll of any single incident.

Unexploded bomb outside 7 Beckington Road, Knowle, 14 April 1943. Dealing with unexploded bombs was an important and dangerous task assigned to the Royal Engineers. This large bomb – Satan – was dropped during the night raid of 3/4 January 1941 and did not explode. It remained buried in Beckington Road for two years until it was recovered from a depth of 29 ft 6 in by Lt Nicholas of the Bomb Disposal Unit, seen on the right. At 8 ft 11 in long without the tail, and weighing 4,000 lb, Satan was the largest bomb dropped on Bristol, and rode in the Victory Parade through London in 1945.

A wartime wedding, 6 March 1943. Jean Brace, a twenty-year-old cigarette packer for W.D. & H.O. Wills, married Ronald Nickless, an RAF pilot, on 6 March 1943 at St Anne's church, Greenbank. The wedding dress was bought with ration coupons from Clark's Bridal Shop in Union Street. Some meat, cakes and tinned fruit were found for the reception before the couple left for three days' honeymoon in Weston-super-Mare.

ARP wardens march past Salmon & Hutchings grocery shop in Shirehampton High Street during victory celebrations i 1945.

VE Day street party in Shirehampton, 8 May 1945. The war was over and people were able to celebrate at last; partie were held in various parts of the city.

ACKNOWLEDGEMENTS

This book would not have been possible without the kind co-operation of John Williams, the City Archivist, and his staff at the Bristol Record Office who have supplied the majority of the photographs. The photographs on pages 162–5 and 270 are from Bristol City Museum & Art Gallery and those on pages 183, 216, 221–21 (top) 256 and 257 are held at the Central Reference Library. Thanks are also due to the Avon & Somerset Constabulary for permission to reproduce the photographs on pages 272 and 273; also to Ivor Aitken for the photograph on page 217; to Mike Hooper for the photographs on pages 231, 240 (top), 247 (top) and 249 (top); and to Denis Williams for the photographs on page 219.

I am indebted to the following for their valuable observations and comments on the text and the photographs: Molly Coghill, Kieran Costello, Paul Elkin, Peter Harris, John Harvey, Mike Hooper, Mike Jenner, Andy King and Karin Walton, and to the staff at Bristol Zoo. I am also grateful to the many people who have given me their time to tell me about life in Bristol between 1920 and 1969. The responsibility for any errors, however, remains my own.

Finally, I would like to thank Simon Fletcher of Sutton Publishing for his enthusiasm and encouragement throughout the project.

BIBLIOGRAPHY

The text of this book has drawn upon a wide range of sources including the spoken record. A wide range of documents was used and some of the most important were building plans, Port of Bristol records, Education Committee records, Minutes of the Housing Committee, Planning Committee documents including the 1952 Development Plan and the 1966 Review, contemporary newspaper accounts, trade catalogues and local directories. The many official guides to the city were useful sources of information, including the Port of Bristol Official Handbooks; most of the local facts and figures quoted in the text are chiefly drawn from such publications. Below is a select bibliography of published works which proved invaluable in the writing of this book.

Anderson, Charles, *A City and its Cinemas*, Redcliffe Press, 1983

Appleby, John B. and other authors, *The People's Carriage 1874–1974*, Bristol Omnibus Company, 1974

Brace, Keith, *Portrait of Bristol*, Robert Hale, 1971

Curtis, M.S., *Bristol, A Century on the Road*, Glasney Press, 1977

Denning, C.F.W., *Old Inns of Bristol*, John Wright & Sons, 1943

Dike, John, *Bristol Blitz Diary*, Redcliffe, 1982

Dresser, Madge, 'People's Housing in Bristol (1870–1939)' in *Bristol's Other History*, Bristol Broadsides, 1983

Elkin, Paul, *Images of Maritime Bristol*, Breedon Books, 1995

English City: The Growth and Future of Bristol, J.S. Fry & Sons, 1945

Hallet, P., *150 Years of Policing in Bristol*, Avon & Somerset Constabulary, 1986

Harrison, David (ed.), *Bristol between the Wars 1919–1939*, Redcliffe Press, 1984

Hasegawa, Junichi, *Replanning the Blitzed City Centre*, OUP, 1992

Lord, J. and Southam, J., *The Floating Harbour*, Redcliffe Press, Bristol, 1983

Penny, J., *The Air Defence of the Bristol Area 1937–44*, Bristol Branch of the Historical Association, 1997

Priest, G. and Cobb, P. (ed.), *The Fight For Bristol*, Bristol Civic Society and Redcliffe, 1980

Priestley, J.B., *English Journey*, Heinemann, 1934

Punter, J.V., *Design Control in Bristol 1940–1990*, Redcliffe, 1990

Ralph, E., *Government of Bristol 1373–1973*, Corporation of Bristol, 1973

Winstone, John, *Bristol As it Was 1963–1975*, Reece Winstone, 1990

Winstone, Reece, *Bristol As it Was 1939–1914*, Reece Winstone, 1978

———. *Bristol 1934–1936*, Reece Winstone, 1986

———. *Bristol in the 1940s*, Reece Winstone, 1970

———. *Bristol 1950–1953*, Reece Winstone, 1970

———. *Bristol 1953– 1956*, Reece Winstone, 1969

———. *Bristol As it Was 1956–1959*, Reece Winstone, 1972

Setright, L.J.K., *Bristol Cars and Engines*, Motor Racing Publications, 1974

Shipley, P., *Bristol Siren Nights*, Rankin Brothers, 1943

Somerville, J., *Christopher Thomas Soapmaker of Bristol*, White Tree Books, 1991

Thomas, Ethel, *Down the Mouth: A History of Avonmouth*, Ethel Thomas, 1977 and 1981

Underdown, T.H.J., *Bristol Under Blitz*, Arrowsmith, 1942

Vear, L., *Bedminster Between the Wars*, Redcliffe, 1981

Vincent, M., *Reflections on the Portishead Branch*, Oxford Publishing Co., 1983

Walker, F., *The Bristol Region*, Thomas Nelson & Sons, 1972

Warne, F.G., *The Bombing of Bristol*, Warne, 1943